SOUPS
AND ONE-POT MEALS

SOUPS
AND
ONE-POT MEALS

THE 100 BEST RECIPES
FROM AROUND THE WORLD

Selected by Christian Teubner

VIKING STUDIO

English language edition produced by
Transedition Limited, 43 Henley Avenue, Oxford,
England.
Published in English in the United States in 1999
by Viking Studio, a member of Penguin Putnam
Inc., 375 Hudson Street, New York, NY 10014,
U.S.A

Published in Germany as *Suppen und Eintöpfe*, in
1998 by Teubner Edition.
Copyright © 1998 Teubner Edition

Translation: Debra Nicol for Translate-A-Book
Editorial: Angela Miccinello and Sue Paruch
Design and production: Richard Johnson
Photography: Christian Teubner, Odette Teubner,
Christian Herr, Ulla Mayer-Raichle, Andreas
Nimptsch, Oliver Schneider
Layout: Christian Teubner, Gabriele Wahl
Origination: Franz Kaufmann GmbH, Stuttgart,
Germany
Printed and bound in the United Arab Emirates
by Emirates Printing Press

Library of Congress Catalog Card Number:
99-75628
ISBN: 0-670-88922-9

10 9 8 7 6 5 4 3 2 1

Contents

Soup, glorious soup

Clear and bound soups, stocks, consommés, and essences

Broadly speaking, soups fall into one of two categories: bound or clear. The former category includes all soups that are thickened with egg yolk, blended, prepared with a béchamel sauce, or fortified with cream. It also includes all "thick soups," as well as stews. A number of these wonderfully tasty recipes (having a further advantage of reducing the number of dishes to wash) are so nourishing that they easily make a complete meal by themselves, or are just perfect for a substantial between-meal snack. By contrast, lighter soups — for example, delicate vegetable soups, but especially clear soups — are traditionally always served at the beginning of a meal or after a cold hors d'oeuvre, which is precisely where they belong; as nourishing as they are tasty — yet light — they tempt the palate and prepare the stomach for pleasures yet to come. Whether talking about bound or clear soups, however, a good stock or broth is essential; many clear soups consist of nothing but stock and a substantial garnish. That's why even though good-quality, prepared stocks can be bought in the grocery store, homemade stock using fresh produce is naturally, as always, the best. A lot of space is devoted to preparing good, fresh stocks over the next few pages, using the most varied ingredients: vegetables as well as meat; veal, beef, or game bones; and the bones and shells of fish and crustaceans. In addition to stocks, also clear are broths and bouillons, the latter having only its name in common with so-called court bouillon, a seasoned stock for poaching fish.

VEGETABLE STOCK
Makes 6½ cups

5 teaspoons butter

2 large white onions, sliced into thick rings

¾ cup broccoli stalks, cut up small

2½ cups chopped leeks, 2¾ cups chopped carrots

1⅔ cups chopped celery, 1 cup chopped zucchini

1⅛ cups white wine, ½ caramelized onion

1 sprig each thyme and rosemary

1 bay leaf, ½ garlic clove, 1 whole clove

Proceed as described in the picture sequence below.

FISH STOCK
Makes 6½ cups

2¼ lb fish bones and trimmings, 3 tablespoons oil

⅔ cup diced shallots, 1½ cups sliced leeks

3½ oz coarsely diced parsley root

⅔ cup diced celery, 2¼ cups white wine

1 bay leaf, 2–3 thyme sprigs

½ teaspoon white peppercorns

Remove the gills and the fins or fin edges. Cut up the fish bones and set aside. Prepare the stock as shown in the picture sequence below.

Preparing fish stock: Soak the bones and trimmings under cold water for about 20 minutes, until the water is clear and free of particles. Drain the bones.

Making a vegetable stock:

Melt the butter in a pot and sauté the onions until lightly browned.

Add the broccoli, leeks, carrots, celery, and zucchini and sauté briefly. Add the wine, simmer, and pour in 3½ qt of water.

Add the caramelized onion; stir in the thyme, rosemary, bay leaf, garlic, and clove; and bring to a boil.

Simmer for 30–40 minutes over low heat, repeatedly skimming off any scum that rises to the surface with a slotted spoon.

Remove from heat and strain the vegetable stock through a conical sieve lined with cheesecloth, reheat, and reduce to 6½ cups.

Sauté the fish bones and trimmings in the oil for 3–4 minutes, stirring frequently, until lightly browned. Add the shallots, leeks, parsley root, and celery and sauté briefly.

As soon as the fish-vegetable mixture begins to simmer, pour in the wine and slowly bring to a boil. Let reduce slightly.

Pour in 9 cups of cold water and reheat slowly. Slow heating is the ideal way to preserve all the flavors.

Add the bay leaf, thyme, and peppercorns. Bring to a boil, carefully (and repeatedly) skimming off any scum that rises to the surface.

Simmer for 20–30 minutes — no longer, or else the consistency becomes gluey. Ladle through a strainer, let cool, and skim off the fat.

Stock — the magic word for good soups

Though sometimes a bit time consuming to prepare, the effort is always worth it

— especially since usually enough stock will be prepared for more than one recipe. Any remaining stock can easily be frozen in batches, so there will always be a supply on hand for the next time soup is made. When preparing stocks, incidentally, they are usually not salted as reducing them later on could make them too salty.

Preparing a light beef stock:
Makes 9 cups. Blanch 4½ lb cleaned, chopped beef bones and 1¼ lb split marrow bones (with the marrow removed). Bring to a boil; drain off the water; and rinse under cold, running water.

Drain the bones well, transfer to a pot, and add enough cold water to cover completely.

Bring to a boil, using a ladle to skim off repeatedly any scum that rises to the surface. Simmer for about 45 minutes.

Add ½ caramelized onion, 2 cloves, 6–8 peppercorns, and a bouquet garni (carrots, leeks, celery, parsley root, garlic, and bay leaf). Simmer for 1½ hours.

Ladle the finished stock through a conical sieve lined with a piece of cheesecloth.

Defat the beef stock once it has cooled completely. To do this, either draw a paper towel carefully across the surface, or skim off the fat with a slotted spoon.

Clarifying a beef stock:

Put 10½ oz beef shin, ⅓ cup carrots, 1 oz parsley root, and ¼ cup celeriac through the coarse blade of a meat grinder, or blend in a food processor.

Mix with ½ caramelized onion, ⅓ cup leeks (cut into rings), 3 allspice berries, 6 peppercorns, 1 bay leaf, 2 cloves, 1 thyme sprig, salt, and 2 egg whites.

Stir in 10 ice cubes. Transfer the mixture to a pot and add 6½–9 cups of cold, defatted, light beef stock.

Bring to a boil, stirring constantly down to the base of the pot so the egg white doesn't burn. Stop stirring as soon as a thick scum rises to the surface.

Simmer for 40–45 minutes. Line a sieve with a piece of cheesecloth and ladle the broth through it, letting it filter through without applying any pressure.

Strong in flavor and absolutely transparent — this is what a perfect consommé should look like. To achieve such a wonderful result, bones are normally used in the stock to intensify its flavor. The stock is then clarified to remove all the particles.

For a completely clear soup, the stock must first be clarified to filter out the particles. In this case, the result is referred to as a consommé: a totally clear, light, but highly aromatic soup, requiring only a delicate garnish for perfection. Essences or fumets are also concentrated in flavor; they are prepared by boiling a clear, or clarified, stock and reducing it down to nothing but flavor, so to speak.

LIGHT CHICKEN STOCK

A few veal bones added to a chicken stock distinctly improve its flavor, as well as making the resulting soup more substantial.

Makes 6½ cups
4½ lb chicken parts (neck, stomach, and heart)
1⅔ lb sliced veal bones, 4 tablespoons oil
1 cup carrots, ⅔ cup celery, both chopped into ½-inch pieces
⅔ cup leeks, ⅓ cup celeriac, both chopped into ½-inch pieces
1⅛ cups dry white wine
1 bay leaf, 15 peppercorns
4 allspice berries, 1 crushed garlic clove

Add the wine and simmer.

Transfer the chicken, bones, and vegetable mixture to a large pot, and add 3½ qt of water.

Bring to a boil, then reduce heat and simmer gently for 2 hours. After 1 hour, add the bay leaf, peppercorns, allspice berries, and garlic. Skim repeatedly.

Remove from heat and let steep for another 20 minutes. Ladle through a conical sieve lined with a piece of cheesecloth.

Let the stock cool and defat by skimming with a slotted spoon or drawing a paper towel across the surface.

Preparing a light chicken stock:
Rinse the chicken parts and veal bones for ½ hour in cold water. Remove and drain well. Heat the oil in a roasting pan and sauté the chicken and bones without letting them brown. Add the carrots, celery, leeks, and celeriac and sauté briefly.

Soup garnishes
Without a garnish, many a soup just isn't complete

For many soups, it is the garnish that truly adds the finishing touch. This is especially true for clear soups, whose charms are evident primarily through the senses of smell and taste. Since eating is also a visual experience though, consommés have

traditionally been supplemented with garnishes. If a stock has been prepared from beef bottom round, for example, using the tender meat as a garnish is as obvious as it is delicate; and julienned vegetables — different varieties cut

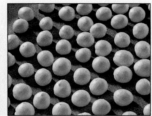

Choux-paste "peas": Preheat the oven to 425°. Bring ½ cup of water to a boil with 2 tablespoons of butter and a little salt. Remove from heat and add ½ cup of flour all at once to the liquid. Stir until the mixture forms a ball. Let cool slightly, then stir in 2 eggs, one at a time. Transfer the dough to a pastry bag, and squeeze pea-sized dots onto a greased and floured baking sheet. Pour 1 cup of water onto the bottom of the oven and bake the "peas" for 10–12 minutes.

Savory custard: Preheat the oven to 215–225°. Crack 5 eggs in a bowl. Whisk in 10 tablespoons of milk and a little salt. Pour this mixture through a fine-mesh sieve, then into a greased 6½ x 6½-inch (or other small) baking pan and cover with aluminum foil. Place in a water bath, then bake for about 30 minutes, until set. Remove from the oven, then loosen the edges all around with a knife and turn out onto a cutting board. Cut into squares or other shapes as desired.

White-bread croutons: Remove the crusts from 4 slices of day-old white bread and cut into uniform, ¼-inch cubes. Melt 7½ teaspoons of butter in a frying pan and sauté until light brown. Remove and lightly season with salt. To make garlic croutons, heat some olive oil in a frying pan, add 1 crushed garlic clove, and sauté until golden brown.

Savory crêpes: Sift 1 cup of flour into a bowl. Add 1⅛ cups of milk, 1 egg, and 1 tablespoon of chopped parsley; stir to a smooth, thin batter. Season with salt and pepper, then let sit for 30 minutes. Melt a little butter in a small (8-inch) frying pan. Make 6 thin crêpes, stacking them on a plate; let cool slightly. Roll up and cut on the diagonal into thin strips.

Marrow dumplings: Finely dice 2 oz of beef marrow. Melt in a saucepan over low heat, then remove from heat and pour through a fine-mesh sieve into a bowl. Let cool. Beat with an electric mixer until frothy, then blend in 2 eggs one after the other. Stir in ¾ cup of fresh bread crumbs, 1 pinch of freshly grated nutmeg, and 1 tablespoon of chopped parsley. Let sit, covered, for 30 minutes. Shape the mixture into small dumplings and simmer gently for 10 minutes in lightly boiling water.

into matchstick strips — make a crunchy and delicious addition to all clear soups. Apart from "reused" ingredients of this type, there are numerous other tasty garnishes, some of which are sold ready-made in supermarkets, delicatessens, and health food stores. Those willing to go to a little extra effort can easily prepare wonderful garnishes themselves, and will soon realize that it is definitely worth the trouble. Garnishes range from plain boiled rice to crunchy bread or airy choux-paste croutons, to pancake strips and savory custard, to dumplings (among the latter, marrow is only one of countless stuffing possibilities). Whether one uses buckwheat flour, semolina, ground meat, or even a delicate fish stuffing as the basis for dumplings, depends entirely on personal preference, the occasion in question, and not the least the soup in which they are to be served. Noodles and pasta also figure prominently among the most popular of soup garnishes. Grocery and health food stores carry special dried pastas in the most varied colors and shapes, made from a truly amazing assortment of ingredients, but why not try some fresh, homemade pasta rather than prepared? It's actually not so difficult, and following the recipe below for a simple, standard pasta dough will guarantee success. Just make sure that all the ingredients are at room temperature, thereby making them easy to work with.

PASTA DOUGH

Makes 14 oz
2⅓ cups wheat flour
3 eggs
1 tablespoon olive oil
½ teaspoon salt

Sift the flour onto a flat surface and make a well in the center. Proceed as shown in the picture sequence opposite.

Crack the eggs into the well, add the olive oil and salt, and stir the contents of the well with a fork.

Gradually stir in more and more flour from the edge, until you have a creamy paste.

Roll out the dough on a flat surface to a uniform thickness. Dust with flour and fold together into a multilayered strip. Slice into ⅛-inch-wide noodles.

Using both hands, heap the remaining flour from the outside over the paste in the middle and knead in.

If it is difficult to knead, mix in about 1 tablespoon of water using both thumbs.

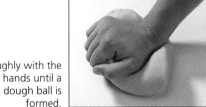

Knead thoroughly with the heels of your hands until a smooth, firm dough ball is formed.

Cover the ball of dough with plastic wrap and let sit for about an hour.

Fish and potato soup

Creamy, but not a cream soup in the true sense, since the potatoes are not puréed in this recipe

The monkfish, also known as the anglerfish, ranks as one of the most highly esteemed inhabitants of the ocean among seafood lovers. The firm consistency of its flesh makes it an ideal garnish for this potato soup. Monkfish is usually sold filleted, since its huge head and fearsome jaws, accounting for almost half of its total length, are of no culinary importance — in marked contrast to the boneless, delicate flesh of the fillet.

Serves 4
1¼ lb monkfish fillet
¼ cup butter
½ cup diced onion, 2 crushed garlic cloves
2¼ lb mealy potatoes, cut into ½-inch cubes
1 teaspoon Hungarian paprika
salt, freshly ground white pepper
3 tablespoons flour, 1 tablespoon oil
½ cup cream, ½ cup milk
For the garnish:
2 hard-boiled eggs, sliced; coarsely ground pepper

1. Rinse the fish fillet briefly under cold water and pat dry. Cut into 1-inch cubes with a sharp knife and refrigerate.

2. Melt half of the butter in a pot and sauté the onion until lightly browned. Add the garlic and potatoes and continue sautéing over medium heat for about 15 minutes, stirring occasionally. Season with paprika, salt, and pepper.

3. Season the fish cubes with salt and dredge them in flour. Heat the oil and the remaining butter in a frying pan and sauté the fish cubes until light brown all over — about 3–4 minutes.

4. Add 1⅛ cups of water to the potatoes and onions and let simmer until the small particles are dissolved. Pour in the cream and milk, and bring to a boil. Reduce heat and simmer for 15–20 minutes. Adjust the seasonings, and add the sautéed fish cubes.

5. Ladle the soup into warmed bowls, garnish with the egg slices, sprinkle with a little coarsely ground pepper, and serve.

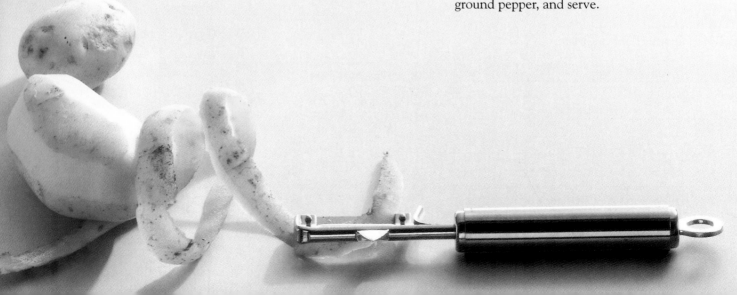

Tomatoes found their way into the national cuisine during the conquest of the New World, in which the Portuguese Crown played no small part; since then, they have become virtually indispensable.

Caldo verde

A cabbage soup that is one of Portugal's national dishes

A special variety of cabbage, *couve galega*, is used in Portugal for this soup. It is cultivated primarily on the *costa verde*, the "green coast" of the country, up to the Minho River, which forms the border with Spain in the north. Farmers frequently plant the cabbage between their grapevines, making optimum use of each patch of fertile soil. *Couve galega* is a long-stemmed brassica, sometimes compared to kale. Unlike kale, though, it does not have ruffled leaves, but instead resembles beet tops or turnip greens. Sold already sliced and packaged in Portuguese markets, *couve galega* is virtually unobtainable outside of the country. For a "Central European" version of *caldo verde*, therefore, Savoy cabbage is recommended, cut into extremely fine strips. A sprinkling of cilantro, which is at least as popular in this type of cooking as parsley, lends a final Portuguese flourish to the soup.

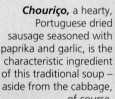

Chouriço, a hearty, Portuguese dried sausage seasoned with paprika and garlic, is the characteristic ingredient of this traditional soup – aside from the cabbage, of course.

Serves 4–6

5¼ cups chicken stock
½ cup diced onion, 1 diced garlic clove
2¼ lb mealy potatoes, cut into cubes
12½ oz Savoy cabbage, sliced into thin strips
salt, freshly ground pepper
For the garnish:
2 tablespoons olive oil
½ cup finely chopped onion, 1 finely chopped garlic clove
7 oz tomatoes, blanched, peeled, seeded, and diced
10½ oz chouriço sausage, skinned and sliced thin
You will also need:
1 tablespoon chopped cilantro leaves

1. Heat the chicken stock in a pot and add the onion, garlic, and potatoes. Bring to a boil. Reduce heat and simmer, covered, for 20 minutes.

2. Rinse the cabbage under cold water and drain well. Set aside.

3. Finely purée the contents of the pot with a handheld blender, then season with salt and pepper. Stir in the cabbage and simmer for 10 minutes.

4. For the garnish, heat the olive oil in a frying pan and sauté the onion and garlic until lightly browned. Add the tomatoes and sausage to the pan and sauté briefly.

5. Ladle the soup into warmed bowls and top with the tomato-sausage mixture. Garnish with cilantro and serve.

Return of the fishing boats: The men bring in their catch as soon as they can. Freshly caught fish and shellfish from the Atlantic represent a good source of income.

Vegetable soup with shellfish

Fresh country bread (*pão*) goes well with this soup, known as *canja de conquilhas* in Portuguese

The bread is guaranteed fresh from the oven when baked at home. Remember, though, to time its baking so it can be served hot with the soup.

Serves 4
For the shellfish court bouillon:
40 razor clams
¾ cup chopped white onion
2 bay leaves, 3 parsley stalks
For the soup:
3 tablespoons olive oil
½ cup finely chopped white onion, 2 finely chopped garlic cloves
1 cup carrots, ⅔ cup leeks, ½ cup celery, all cut into thin, 2-inch strips
10 saffron threads, salt, freshly ground pepper
⅓ cup long-grain rice
1 egg yolk and 1 tablespoon lemon juice, mixed together
1 tablespoon chopped parsley
For the country bread:
1⅔ cups white flour
2⅓ cups whole wheat flour
1 fresh yeast cake (about 1⅓ oz)
½ teaspoon salt, olive oil

Razor clams can be quite sandy, so they should be washed thoroughly before cooking.

1. To make the court bouillon, soak the razor clams in cold water for 10 minutes, then rinse thoroughly under cold water. Bring 6½ cups of water to a boil in a large pot and add the onion, bay leaves, and parsley stalks. Add the razor clams and boil lightly until they open. Remove the clams from the boiling water and shuck two-thirds of them. Pour the hot liquid from the pot through a fine sieve and set aside 4 cups.

2. To make the soup, heat the olive oil in a pot and sauté the onion and garlic until translucent. Add the carrots, leeks, and celery and sauté briefly. Pour in the bouillon, add the saffron threads, and season with salt and pepper. Bring to a boil and sprinkle in the rice. Reduce heat and simmer for 15 minutes. Add the shucked and unshucked razor clams and simmer for another 5 minutes.

3. Remove from heat — it shouldn't come to a boil — and stir in the egg yolk mixture. Adjust the seasonings, ladle the soup into heated bowls, sprinkle with parsley, and serve.

For the bread, combine the two types of flour in a large bowl; make a well in the center and crumble in the yeast. Mix the yeast with 1½ cups of lukewarm water and a little flour. Dust this "starter" with flour, cover, and let rise for 15 minutes. Add the salt, knead to a smooth dough, and roll into a ball. Brush the inside of a bowl with olive oil and turn in the dough until coated. Cover and let rise for about an hour. Preheat the oven to 390–400⁰. Knead the dough thoroughly and shape into a round loaf, about 8 inches in diameter. Place the loaf on a lightly oiled baking sheet, cover, and let rise for 20 minutes. Bake for 40–45 minutes.

Pescados y mariscos, fish and seafood, abound in Spain's numerous fish markets. Here, the much-sought-after hake is on sale.

Hake and tomato soup

Spain's coastal regions are famous for their delicious soups with fish

Light and refreshing, the combination of tomatoes and fish is a popular one in Spain. Many variations on this theme are used, often containing a wide variety of shellfish — one need only think of zarzuela, the Catalonian seafood stew. *Merluza* (hake) is the preferred fish for this fruity, slightly sharp, tomato soup — on the one hand because its flesh is especially tasty, firm, and lean, on the other because it has very few bones. If hake is unavailable, however, codfish or haddock make good substitutes.

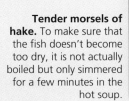

Tender morsels of hake. To make sure that the fish doesn't become too dry, it is not actually boiled but only simmered for a few minutes in the hot soup.

Serves 4
1 gutted hake, with the skin on (about 2¼ lb)
juice of 1 lemon
2 tablespoons olive oil
2 cups finely chopped onion
1 finely chopped garlic clove
½ teaspoon fennel seeds
2⅔ cups fish stock
½ cup dry white wine
1½ lb fresh tomatoes, blanched, skinned, seeded, and chopped
salt, freshly ground white pepper

For the garnish:
1 bunch finely chopped parsley

1. Carefully wash the gutted fish inside and out under cold water, then pat dry with paper towels. Using a cloth, hold firmly at the tail end and cut off the fins, working toward the head. Remove the head by cutting diagonally into the fish on both sides, right behind the gill opening, toward the head as far as the central bone. To detach the fillets, cut with a sharp knife along the backbone up to the central bone, slide the knife at an angle

under the top fillet, and cut off in the direction of the tail. Carefully lift the fillets off the bones, making sure all the small bones have been removed; this is most easily done with tweezers. Slice into bite-sized chunks, drizzle both sides with lemon juice, and refrigerate.

2. Heat the olive oil in a large pot. Add the onion, garlic, and fennel seeds and sauté briefly, stirring continuously. Pour in the fish stock and the wine and add the tomatoes. Bring to a boil, cover, and simmer for about 10 minutes over low heat.

3. Season the soup with salt and pepper. Carefully transfer the hake pieces to the pot, cover, and simmer over low heat for 4–5 minutes.

4. Ladle the soup into bowls, garnish with parsley, and serve.

Almonds, here freshly picked, were once brought by the Moors to Spain where they now feature prominently in Spanish cuisine. Indispensable for cookies and other baking, they are also used in sauces and soups.

Sopa de almendras

This almond soup with garlic and saffron is a specialty from Granada

Almond soups, usually referred to as "white gazpachos," are especially popular in southern Spain. The majority are enjoyed ice cold, as a pleasantly refreshing meal in the sweltering summer heat — a version from Málaga, with garlic and white grapes, has become especially well known. The following soup, on the other hand, is completely different; it can be eaten hot and is thus also very tasty on cold, winter days.

Serves 4

1½ cups whole almonds, 4 tablespoons olive oil

3–4 slices day-old white bread, cut into cubes

Saffron threads and sweet red peppers give the soup its lovely yellow color. After peeling, the almonds are briefly roasted in olive oil further to intensify their flavor.

4 chopped garlic cloves

1⅓ cups sweet red peppers, chopped into ½-inch pieces

coarse salt, freshly ground black pepper

½ teaspoon saffron threads

1 tablespoon chopped parsley

For the garnish:

¼ cup roasted, flaked almonds

a little chopped peppermint, mint sprigs

1. Scald the almonds with boiling water in a bowl; let sit briefly, then pour off the hot water. Rinse with ice-cold water, peel off the skins, and pat dry.

2. Heat half of the olive oil in a frying pan and roast the almonds over medium to high heat, stirring frequently until they turn light brown. Remove, drain on paper towels, and set aside.

3. Heat the remaining olive oil in the pan and sauté the bread cubes until golden brown, stirring constantly. Add the garlic and red pepper and sauté for 2 minutes. Season with salt and pepper, sprinkle in the saffron threads, and remove from heat.

4. In a food processor or blender, combine the roasted almonds and the bread-pepper mixture with ¾ cup of water and blend to a fine paste.

5. Bring 3¾ cups of water to a boil in a large pot. Stir in the paste bit by bit, until it is completely blended with the water, and simmer over low heat for 10 minutes. Stir in the parsley and adjust the seasonings.

6. Ladle the soup into 4 bowls. Garnish each with the roasted, flaked almonds; chopped peppermint; and a sprig of mint and serve.

Sopes mallorquines

A vegetable stew from Majorca — a rustic dish containing plenty of cabbage, crusty bread, and sausage

On Majorca this delicious dish can be made in different ways, with either *sobrasada* — a typically Majorcan, pâté-like, soft, paprika sausage — or some other type of meat. Since *sobrasada* is not widely available, a Spanish variant on this soup, with chorizo (hot, paprika sausage) and Rioja (red wine) is given.

Serves 4
1⅓ lb white cabbage, sliced into thin strips
6 tablespoons olive oil
1 cup finely chopped onion
2 finely chopped garlic cloves
1 lb ripe tomatoes, blanched, skinned, seeded, and diced
salt, freshly ground pepper
4½ cups vegetable stock
For the soup pots:
7 oz crusty bread (e.g., French baguette), sliced thin
½ cup Rioja
3½ oz chorizo sausage, skinned and sliced thin
For the garnish:
1 tablespoon chopped herbs (thyme, parsley, etc.)

1. Rinse the cabbage briefly under cold water. Place in a pot of boiling, salted water and let boil for 10–12 minutes, until almost tender. Drain well and set aside.

2. Heat the olive oil in a pot and sauté the onion and garlic without letting them brown. Add the tomatoes and sauté briefly; season with salt and pepper. Pour in the vegetable stock and bring to a boil. Reduce heat and simmer for 15 minutes. Adjust the seasonings and keep warm.

3. Preheat the oven to 390–400⁰. Line the bottom of 4 ovenproof (clay) pots with bread slices, drizzle with the Rioja, and top with a layer of chorizo and white cabbage. Repeat this process two more times for each pot, finishing with a layer of bread.

4. Ladle the soup into the pots and garnish with the herbs. Bake for approximately 10 minutes. Remove from the oven and serve while piping hot.

On the island of Majorca this hearty dish is served in rustic ceramic pots. If these are unavailable, normal soup cups may be used without any adverse effect on the flavor.

Spanish *morcilla*, blood sausage with lots of onion, is a classic ingredient of the *fabada*. It is not a coincidence that the best *morcillas* come from Asturias and Estremadura.

Asturian bean stew

Called *fabada*, this stew is a favorite well beyond the borders of its native province of Asturias

The most important ingredient of this tasty stew, which originated in the mountains of Cantabria (the western extension of the Pyrénées), is the large, mild, white beans — known in Spain as *habas* or favas. These are soaked overnight, before being simmered slowly over a *low* heat — this is important, as they would otherwise split — together with the bacon, aromatic serrano ham, and pig's foot, until soft. On the other hand, the two varieties of sausage — chorizo and *morcilla* (Spanish blood sausage) — are not added until the end, as they only require warming through in the hot sauce.

A hearty stew that owes its gutsy flavor to two different kinds of sausage — plus bacon, ham, and pork. Not the lightest of dishes, but typically Spanish all the same.

Serves 4
12½ oz large, white, dried beans
1 tablespoon olive oil
¾ cup finely chopped onion, 3 finely chopped garlic cloves
3 oz uncooked smoked bacon, cut into small cubes
3½ oz serrano ham, cut into small cubes
2 tablespoons tomato paste
1 tablespoon Hungarian paprika
1 pig's foot (about 1½ lb), chopped crosswise into 3–4 pieces
2 bay leaves
salt, freshly ground black pepper
8½ oz chorizo sausage
8½ oz morcilla sausage
For the garnish:
1 tablespoon chopped parsley

1. Rinse the beans under cold water, place in a bowl with enough cold water to cover, and let soak overnight. The next day, rinse the beans under cold water and drain well. Set aside.

2. Heat the olive oil in a pot and sauté the onion and garlic until lightly browned. Add the bacon and ham and sauté for 3–4 minutes. Stir in the tomato paste and sauté briefly. Sprinkle over the paprika (taking care to not let it burn, thereby making it bitter), pour in 6½ cups of water, and bring to a boil.

3. Add the pig's foot pieces to the pot. Add the beans and bay leaves and season with salt and pepper. Reduce heat and simmer for about 1½ hours, repeatedly skimming off the scum that rises to the surface.

4. In the final 5 minutes of cooking time, add the chorizo and *morcilla* and heat slowly. Remove the sausage, slice into bite-sized pieces, and add them back to the pot. Adjust the seasonings, garnish with parsley, and serve.

Cold vegetable soup

Made from tomatoes, bell peppers, and cucumbers, blended together and chilled well — delightfully refreshing

Serves 4
about 2 slices white bread, crusts removed
⅔ cup diced white onion, 2 diced garlic cloves
2 tablespoons olive oil, salt, freshly ground pepper
1⅓ lb tomatoes, blanched, skinned, and quartered
2 cups diced sweet red pepper
1⅔ cups cucumber, peeled, seeded, and diced
1–2 tablespoons sherry vinegar
2¼ cups chilled, defatted meat stock
For the garnish:
3 tablespoons olive oil
about 3–4 slices crustless white bread, cut into ¼-inch cubes
1 diced garlic clove
salt, 12 green olives, pitted and halved
½ cup finely chopped white onion
1 tablespoon chopped borage leaves, a few borage flowers

Olive harvest means manual labor: With the aid of a small rake the olives are carefully "combed" from the tree, branch by branch, falling onto a net spread out on the ground below.

Suitable garnishes for this cold vegetable soup are freshly made white-bread croutons, onions, olives, and (a particularly attractive touch) borage flowers.

1. Dip the bread slices in water and gently squeeze dry. Put the onion and garlic in a blender with the bread. Pour in the olive oil, season with salt and pepper, and blend until very smooth.

2. Scoop out the seeds from the tomatoes and strain through a sieve, pressing with the back of a spoon, and collecting the juices in a bowl. Chop the remaining tomatoes.

3. Add the chopped tomatoes, red pepper, cucumber, reserved tomato juice, and sherry vinegar to the bread mixture in the blender and purée until very smooth; do this in several batches if necessary.

Large green olives are a popular snack in tapas bars along with a glass of wine; but they also taste wonderful in a fruity, slightly sharp soup, as here.

4. Transfer the purée to a bowl, adjust the seasonings, and chill in the refrigerator for a couple of hours (better still, overnight). The next day, stir in the defatted meat stock.

5. For the garnish, heat the olive oil in a frying pan and sauté the bread cubes and garlic until golden. Drain on paper towels and salt lightly. Ladle the chilled soup into bowls and garnish with bread cubes, olives, white onion, and borage leaves and flowers.

Breton fishermen bring in sought-after, prime-quality seafood — highly esteemed by gourmets, who know that langoustine quality largely depends on freshness.

Bisque de langoustines

One of the great classics of French cuisine, with choice lobsters — a sheer delight

Serves 4

8 langoustines (small lobsters, about 5 oz each)

3 tablespoons olive oil, 2 tablespoons butter

¼ cup leeks, ½ cup carrots, ¼ cup celery, ⅔ cup onions, ¼ cup shallots, 2 small garlic cloves

⅓ cup blanched long-grain rice, 2 tablespoons tomato paste, ½ cup white wine, ½ cup Noilly Prat vermouth, ⅛ cup cognac, 5¼ cups fish stock

1 sprig tarragon, 1 sprig each parsley and basil, salt, cayenne pepper

⅓ cup heavy cream

For the garnish:

5 teaspoons butter, 2 tablespoons olive oil

½ cup blanched julienned leeks, ¼ cup blanched julienned celery

1 tarragon sprig, salt, cayenne pepper, 1 tablespoon chopped tarragon

1. Twist off the langoustine tails, remove the meat, and refrigerate. Remove the

intestine (the dark thread), which must not tear. Halve the head sections and wash them out carefully; only the shells will be used. Chop all the shells into small pieces.

2. Heat the olive oil and butter and sauté the shells for 10 minutes. Add the leeks, carrots, celery, onion, shallots, and garlic and sauté for 5 minutes. Add the rice; sauté until translucent. Stir in the tomato paste and sauté for 2–3 minutes. Add the wine and simmer, pour in the vermouth and cognac, and reduce the liquid by half. Add the fish stock, tarragon, parsley, and basil and bring to a boil. Simmer over low heat for 20–25 minutes.

3. Remove from heat and purée. Strain through a fine-mesh sieve, pressing down hard on the ingredients while straining. Return to heat, season with salt and cayenne pepper, and keep warm.

4. Heat the butter and olive oil for the garnish and sauté the tarragon sprig. Season the tail meat with salt and cayenne pepper, and fry until golden brown. Sprinkle with the chopped tarragon.

5. Whip the cream until it forms soft peaks, gently fold into the bisque. Spoon the tail meat, leeks, and celery into soup cups, ladle in the bisque, and garnish with the fried tarragon. Serve at once.

This delectable cream of seafood soup is enriched with cognac and seasoned with cayenne pepper. The cream — whipped to perfection — is folded in gently only at the very end.

Cream of artichoke soup

The hearts of the artichoke are served here in a surprisingly different way — as a creamy soup

Serves 4
12 artichokes with stalks (about 7 oz each)
2 tablespoons lemon juice
½ sliced lemon, 1 teaspoon salt, 3 tablespoons butter
½ cup diced shallots, 1 diced garlic clove
8½ oz chopped mealy potatoes
salt, white pepper
⅓ cup heavy cream blended with ⅓ teaspoon buttermilk (créme fraîche)
You will also need:
¼ cup heavy cream, 1 tablespoon chopped parsley

1. Cut the prickly outer leaves off each artichoke stalk and discard. Break the stalk off underneath the head. Gently strip off the small, tough leaves around the base of the stalk, snip off the prickly tips of the leaves, and discard. Cut off the tip of each artichoke and immediately place in water with the juice of half a lemon.

Once an artichoke has been trimmed and boiled, there's not much left to eat — just the flesh of the outer leaves and the heart. Both, however, are popular with epicures, owing to their delicately tangy, slightly bitter flavor.

2. Bring about 3½ qt of water to a boil in a large pot with the lemon juice, lemon slices, and salt. Add the artichokes, reduce heat, and simmer for 20–25 minutes. Remove from heat, take out the artichokes, and rinse. Save the cooking liquid. Remove the leaves from the cooked artichokes and save for another recipe or use as a garnish with vinaigrette dressing. Scoop out and discard the hairy "choke" of each artichoke. Dice the artichoke hearts and set aside.

3. Heat the butter and sauté the shallots and garlic without letting them brown. Add the

potatoes, pour over 4½ cups of the cooking liquid, and simmer over low heat for 10 minutes. Add the artichoke hearts, season with salt and pepper, and simmer for another 10–15 minutes.

4. Remove from heat and purée until smooth. Stir in the crème fraîche, blend briefly, and adjust the seasonings. Whip the cream until it forms soft peaks. Ladle into bowls, garnish with whipped cream, and sprinkle with parsley. Serve.

Clear oxtail soup

This famous clear, amber broth derives its unmistakable character from sherry and balsamic vinegar

Serves 4

1¾ lb oxtail meat, ½ cup butter

3 lb cut-up veal bones and beef bones

1⅔ cups onion, 1 cup carrots, ⅔ cup celery, ¾ cup leeks, all coarsely chopped

1 tablespoon tomato paste, 3¼ cups white wine

1 sprig each thyme, rosemary, sage, parsley, and basil

For clarifying the stock:

1½ whole carrots, 2 oz parsley root

14 oz beef, ¾ cup sliced leeks, 2 cloves

3 allspice berries, 10 white peppercorns

1 sprig each thyme, rosemary, and basil

½ teaspoon marjoram, 2 garlic cloves, 1 bay leaf

5 egg whites, 10 ice cubes

You will also need:

1 tablespoon vinegar, 2 tablespoons dry sherry, salt

Cut through the oxtail meat at the joints. Proceed as shown in the photo sequence on the right. When the meat is done — 3–3½ hours — remove, strip the meat from the bones, let cool, and dice. Strain the stock, let cool, and defat. The stock is then clarified as follows: Coarsely grind all the ingredients in a blender or food processor. Place the mixture in a pot with the cold beef stock and bring to a boil, stirring down to the base of the pot so the egg white doesn't stick. Stop stirring when a dense scum rises to the surface. Simmer for 40–45 minutes. Line a sieve with cheesecloth; pour in the broth and let it run through freely. Return the meat to the soup and heat through. Before serving, season with vinegar, sherry, and a little salt.

Preheat the oven to 350°. Melt the butter in a roasting pan. Add the oxtail, veal bones and beef bones, onion, carrots, celery, and leeks and roast in the oven, letting the liquid simmer.

Stir the contents of the pan several times, letting it brown. When the liquid has evaporated completely, add the tomato paste and dry-roast.

Pour in the wine bit by bit, allowing it to evaporate between each addition. (By doing this, the tomato paste loses its sweetness and deepens in color.)

Once the wine is reduced, pour in enough cold water to cover the bones; add the thyme, rosemary, sage, parsley, and basil sprigs. Simmer gently, uncovered, on the stove.

This classic soup only becomes completely transparent when clarified with lean beef and egg whites. Finely diced oxtail meat makes the ideal garnish.

Oscietra caviar, known in Russian as *ossiotr,* is a favorite of caviar connoisseurs — understandably so, as the nutty flavor of the small, hard-shelled roe is incomparable. It comes from the *oscietra* sturgeon, which can weigh over 450 pounds, although its average weight is about 175 pounds. Only a few minutes elapse from the time the roe is removed from an anesthetized sturgeon to the time it is packaged — it could hardly be fresher!

Fine potato soups
Served cold with delectable garnishes — exquisite appetizers for the warm, summer months

VICHYSSOISE

Serves 4
1lb mealy potatoes, cut into cubes, salt
¼ cup lukewarm milk
5 teaspoons melted butter
freshly ground white pepper
freshly grated nutmeg
3¼ cups strong beef stock
7½ teaspoons heavy cream blended with dash buttermilk (crème fraîche)
You will also need:
8 quail's eggs
⅓ cup heavy cream, 1 tablespoon chopped chives
1 small (1-oz) jar oscietra caviar

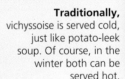

Traditionally, vichyssoise is served cold, just like potato-leek soup. Of course, in the winter both can be served hot.

1. Boil the potatoes in lightly salted water until soft, then drain well and purée while still warm. Put the puréed potatoes in a bowl; whisk in the milk and butter; and season with salt, pepper, and nutmeg.

2. Bring the beef stock to a boil in a pot. Whisk in the potato purée and the crème fraîche and simmer for 10 minutes over low heat. Remove from heat and let cool, stirring frequently. Set aside.

3. Boil the quail's eggs for 7 minutes. Carefully remove, rinse under cold water, then peel and halve lengthwise. Set aside. Whip the cream until it forms soft peaks.

4. Mix the cooled soup with a blender, then fold in the cream and sprinkle in the chives. Ladle into soup plates, garnish with 4 egg halves, spoon the caviar on top, and serve.

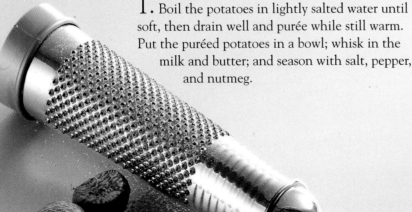

COLD POTATO-LEEK SOUP

Serves 4 (not pictured)

3 tablespoons butter

10½ oz sliced mealy potatoes

salt, freshly ground white pepper

10 teaspoons white wine, 3¼ cups vegetable stock

4–5oz fresh herbs (parsley, chervil, tarragon, and dill), leaves only

8½ oz leeks, halved lengthwise and sliced; 1 teaspoon lemon juice, 1 teaspoon balsamic vinegar

2–3 drops Tabasco

⅔ cup heavy cream blended with ⅔ teaspoon buttermilk (crème fraîche)

1. Melt half of the butter in a pot and sauté the potatoes without letting them brown. Add the salt, pepper, wine, and vegetable stock and simmer over low heat.

2. Blend the herbs to a fine purée with the remaining butter and refrigerate.

3. Add the leeks to the soup and simmer for about 10 minutes, then remove from heat and purée in a blender. Add the chilled herb butter and blend thoroughly once more. Strain through a fine-mesh sieve and season with lemon juice, balsamic vinegar, and Tabasco. Cool thoroughly. Serve well chilled, adding the crème fraîche at the last minute.

Alsatian lentil soup

A hearty lentil stew, served with crusty bread and a glass of Sylvaner — a typical meal for this region of eastern France

Alsatian cervelas is the best accompaniment for a potage (thick soup) *au lentilles à l'Alsacienne*. These frankfurter-style sausages, made of beef with bacon, bacon rind, and spices, derive their typical flavor from an hour-long stay in a *fumoir* (smoking room). If cervelas cannot be found, they may be replaced by any other ring-shaped, smoked sausage.

Serves 4

¾ cup small, brown lentils
1 tablespoon vegetable oil
⅔ cup diced uncooked bacon
½ cup diced onion, 1 diced garlic clove
2¼ cups carrots, diced into ¼-inch cubes
10½ oz potatoes, diced into ¼-inch cubes
1½ cups leeks, sliced ¼-inch thick
2 tablespoons chopped parsley
2 cloves, 1 bay leaf
salt, freshly ground pepper
6½ cups beef stock
You will also need:
10½ oz cervelas, skinned and sliced thin
1 tablespoon chopped parsley

1. Pour the lentils into a colander or sieve and rinse under cold water. Place in a bowl with enough fresh water to cover and let soak overnight. The following day, drain well and set aside.

2. Heat the vegetable oil in a large pot and sauté the bacon, onion, and garlic until translucent. Add the carrots, potatoes, and leeks, and continue to sauté for 3–4 minutes.

3. Add the parsley, cloves, and bay leaf, and season with salt and pepper. Add the beef stock and drained lentils and bring to a boil. Reduce heat and simmer for 45 minutes.

4. Remove from heat and take out the cloves and bay leaf. Blend half of the soup in batches until smooth in a blender, then pour back into the pot with the remaining soup.

5. Stir in the sausage. Reheat and simmer for another 5 minutes. Ladle the soup into soup plates and serve sprinkled with parsley.

To filter the juice, decant the puréed tomato into the center of a clean cheesecloth, draw the four corners together at the top, and tie with string. Suspend the bag over a bowl to catch the juice.

Tomato essence with monkfish

The classic way to serve this recipe is cold, but it also tastes superb as a hot soup

It is recommended that the tomato essence be made the day before it will be served, since the preparation process is a lengthy one. Only if the essence is allowed to drip through a cloth over several hours without the application of any external pressure will it be completely clear, thus becoming the basis for a slightly gelled, refreshing summer soup.

The monkfish fillet is coated with pesto and gently baked in the oven, producing a succulent, tender result that perfectly complements the flavor of the basil sauce.

Serves 4
For the tomato essence:
3 lb ripe tomatoes, cored and diced; ¼ cup diced celery
½ cup diced onion, 2 diced garlic cloves
1 oz fresh basil leaves
10 peppercorns
½ teaspoon coarse sea salt
1 teaspoon gelatin dissolved in cold water
For the pesto:
1 tablespoon pine nuts
1 coarsely chopped garlic clove, salt
1 oz coarsely chopped fresh basil leaves
⅛ cup extra virgin olive oil
You will also need:
7 oz monkfish fillet
1 tablespoon olive oil, for greasing the baking pan
3 tablespoons fish stock, 3½ oz tomatoes, blanched, skinned, seeded, and thinly sliced
basil leaves for garnishing

1. Combine the tomatoes, celery, onion, garlic, basil leaves, peppercorns, and salt in a blender or food processor and blend until smooth.

2. Strain the puréed tomato through a cheesecloth over a bowl, allowing it to drip through without applying any pressure, as shown in the photo above left. (The cloth bag can be hung from a broomstick held in place horizontally, or suspended from the legs of an upended chair.) This should yield about 3¼ cups of liquid.

3. Stir the dissolved gelatin into the tomato essence. Cool the mixture in the refrigerator until it starts to gel slightly.

4. For the pesto, if desired, first toast the pine nuts briefly in a dry, heavy pan — this brings out their flavor.

5. Using a mortar and pestle, grind the garlic, salt, and pine nuts to a paste. Add the basil leaves and mix well. Slowly add the olive oil in a thin trickle, stirring it in carefully. Set aside.

6. Preheat the oven to 350º. Rinse the monkfish fillet briefly under cold water and gently pat dry. Brush on all sides with pesto. Grease an ovenproof dish with olive oil and layer in the monkfish fillet. Bake for about 10 minutes, adding the fish stock after 5 minutes. Remove the fillet from the oven and let cool slightly.

7. Ladle the tomato essence into soup cups. Cut the fillet crosswise into 4 strips and add to the soup cups, together with the tomato slices. Serve garnished with basil.

Bell peppers *(Capsicum annuum* var. *annuum)* grow on the upright, bushy capsicum plant, which flowers and fruits continously so that the harvesting of the berry takes place over a long period of time. All peppers go through an initial green, unripe stage. If left on the plant until completely ripened, they turn yellow or red.

Sweet-pepper soup
The sky's the creative limit when you prepare this soup in different colors

To introduce a colorful note to a fairly large dinner party, an additional quantity of the following recipe — which serves 4 — can be prepared using yellow peppers. If a half-quantity of the soup is also then prepared with green peppers, varied effects can be achieved by ladling a dollop of one color into a bowl of another color. If a strongly flavored soup with an intense color is preferred, keep the skins on the peppers. Skinned peppers, on the other hand, give the soup a more delicate taste and allow the basic flavors to shine through. In addition to chicken stock, veal, beef, or fish stock are suitable for this recipe.

dollop of a different color, and decorate as desired by swirling with a fork.

Heat the oil in a pot and sauté the shallots with the sugar.

Stir in the lemon juice and stew the pepper strips for 5 minutes, stirring occasionally.

Pour in the chicken stock, bring to a boil, and simmer for 10 minutes. Add the cream and simmer for another 5 minutes.

Add the garlic, ginger, thyme, parsley, and rosemary. Season with salt, pepper, and ginger and continue to simmer.

Remove from heat and take out the herbs and garlic with a slotted spoon. Blend the soup until smooth and pour through a strainer.

Serves 4
1¾ lb sweet peppers of the same color
3 tablespoons oil
½ cup finely chopped shallots, 1 teaspoon sugar
2 tablespoons lemon juice, 2¼ cups chicken stock
½ cup heavy cream, 1 crushed garlic clove
about ¼ oz freshly grated ginger
1 sprig each thyme, parsley, and rosemary tied together with a string
1 teaspoon salt
freshly ground white pepper, ground ginger

Preheat the oven to 425⁰. Wash and skin the peppers. To do this, roast them until their skins turn brown and blister. Remove from the oven, place under a damp cloth or in a plastic bag, and let sweat. Pull off the skin in strips, from top to bottom. Halve the peppers lengthwise, remove the seeds and membranes, and cut them into strips. Prepare the soup as described in the picture sequence. Reheat the soup before serving. If the basic recipe has been prepared in several colors, place a ladleful of one color in a bowl, add a

Vermouth is made from wine and the bitter essences of the wormwood shrub. The Noilly Prat business in Marseilles is reputed to have invented French vermouth. The drink is aged outdoors in oak barrels for five years, which gives it its distinctive flavor. It is available in Blanc, Rouge, Extra Dry, and French Dry varieties, the latter in particular playing an important role in French gourmet cuisine.

Saffron fish soup
White wine and vermouth impart a delectable flavor; saffron, a beautiful color

The basis of this fine, French fish soup is a homemade stock. To save time, however, a good-quality, prepared fish stock available in grocery or health food stores can also be used.

Serves 4
For the fish stock:
1⅛ lb white-fleshed fish
2 tablespoons vegetable oil
⅓ cup diced shallots, ¾ cup sliced leeks (white part only)
½ cup chopped parsley root, ⅓ cup chopped celery
1 cup white wine, 10 teaspoons Noilly Prat vermouth
1 bay leaf, 1–2 thyme sprigs
¼ teaspoon white peppercorns
For the garnish:
3½ oz monkfish fillet
3½ oz fillet of sole
3½ oz salmon fillet
salt, freshly ground pepper
¼ cup shallots, ⅓ cup leeks (white part only), both cut into 2-inch-long julienne strips
1 small (1-oz) parsley root, ⅛ cup celery, both cut into 2-inch-long julienne strips
⅓ cup carrots, cut into 2-inch-long julienne strips
3 tablespoons vegetable oil
You will also need:
a few saffron threads
¼ cup ice-cold butter, cut into small pieces
a few dill sprigs

Adding ⅓ cup of heavy cream 10 minutes before the end of cooking time and simmering before whisking in the ice-cold butter adds an extra touch of class and lavishness to the soup.

1. To make the stock, remove the gills from the fish heads and coarsely chop the remaining body. Rinse under cold water, until it is free from cloudy substances; drain thoroughly.

2. Heat the vegetable oil in a large pan and sauté the chopped fish for 3–4 minutes until lightly

browned. Add the shallots, leeks, parsley root, and celery and sauté briefly, turning frequently. As soon as the mixture begins to simmer, add the wine and the vermouth; heat slowly and allow to evaporate slightly. Pour in 4½ cups of water; add the bay leaf, thyme, and peppercorns, and bring to a boil. Reduce heat and simmer for 20–30 minutes, repeatedly skimming off any scum that forms. Remove from heat. Line a conical sieve with a piece of cheesecloth, pour in the stock, and allow it to run through freely. There should be 4½ cups of stock remaining. Set aside.

3. For the garnish, briefly rinse all the fish fillets under cold water and pat dry with paper towels.

Cut into 1-inch pieces, then season with salt and pepper. Set aside. Blanch the shallots, leeks, parsley root, celery, and carrots in boiling, salted water for 1–2 minutes. Drain and set aside.

4. Heat the vegetable oil for the garnish in a pan, fry the fish pieces for 1–2 minutes on all sides, and remove. Drain on paper towels and set aside.

5. Reheat the stock, then sprinkle in the saffron threads and adjust the seasonings. Add the butter and blend with a handheld blender. Arrange the fish chunks and vegetables in warmed bowls and ladle in the soup. Garnish with dill and serve at once.

The term "confit" refers to pieces of goose, duck, or pork preserved in salt and fat. This traditional preserving method is a special process from the southwest of France. Confit is frequently served cold, but is also an essential ingredient in such classic dishes as cassoulet (white bean and meat casserole) or *garbure*.

Garbure

A Gascon stew with three kinds of meat, vegetables, and fresh herbs

Although *garbure* originated in Gascony, a province in southwestern France, numerous versions of this vegetable stew have become popular in many of the regional cuisines of that country. A typically Gascon approach is to prepare it with confit (meat that has been cooked and preserved in its own fat). Additionally, Gascons who still follow their culinary heritage leave a bit of broth in the bowl and wash it down with red wine. In the local dialect, this little ritual is known as *le chabrot*. In many places in France, people cook the potatoes and vegetables for the *garbure* separately, then layer them in a tureen, alternating with meat. The dish is then seasoned with freshly ground pepper, sprinkled with cheese, and gratinéed in the oven.

Before serving, place a slice of bread in each bowl, ladle in the vegetable stew, and sprinkle with parsley.

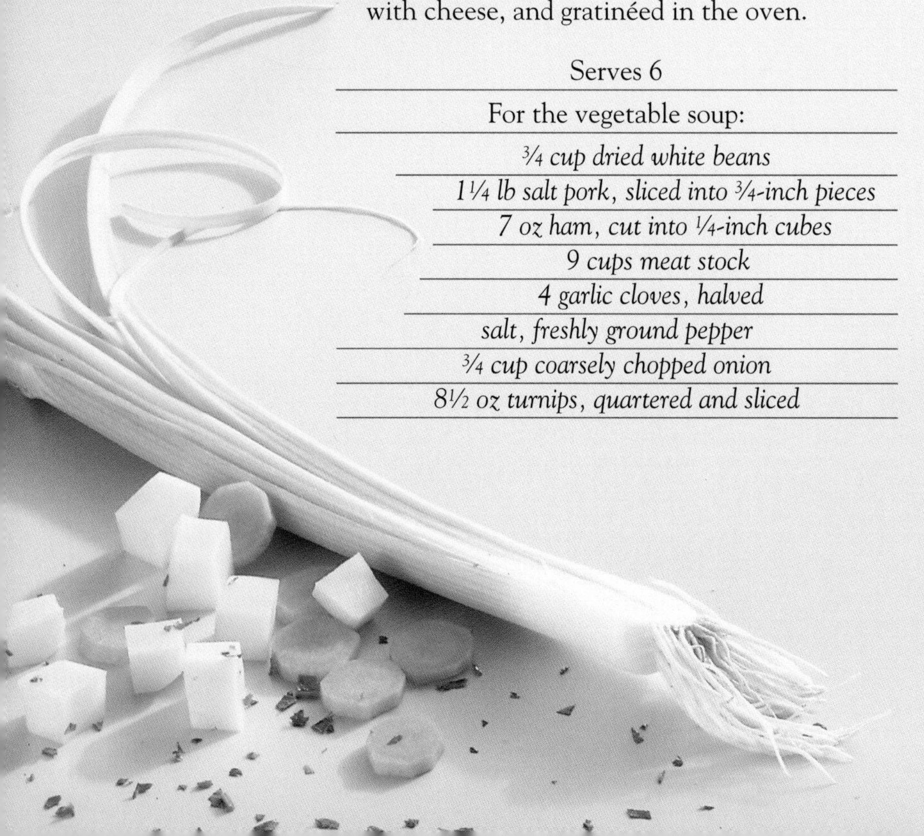

Serves 6
For the vegetable soup:
¾ cup dried white beans
1¼ lb salt pork, sliced into ¾-inch pieces
7 oz ham, cut into ¼-inch cubes
9 cups meat stock
4 garlic cloves, halved
salt, freshly ground pepper
¾ cup coarsely chopped onion
8½ oz turnips, quartered and sliced

1¾ cups sliced carrots
¾ cup sliced leeks
⅔ cup sliced celery
1¼ lb potatoes, chopped into ¾-inch pieces
10½ oz white cabbage, cut into bite-sized pieces
For the bouquet garni:
1 bay leaf
3 sprigs parsley
1 sprig each thyme and oregano
1 sprig rosemary
You will also need:
a few pieces diced goose confit
1 tablespoon chopped parsley
sliced French bread

1. Place the beans in a bowl with enough cold water to cover and let soak overnight. The next day, pour off the water and drain well.

2. Place the pork, ham, and beans in a pot and cover with the meat stock; bring to a boil. Reduce heat, add the bouquet garni and garlic, and season with salt and pepper. Simmer very gently for 40 minutes.

3. Add the onion, turnips, carrots, leeks, celery, and potatoes and stir well together; simmer for another 15 minutes. Add the white cabbage and the goose confit, and simmer for an additional

20–25 minutes or until all ingredients are tender. Adjust the seasonings, garnish with parsley, and serve with the French bread.

Meat stew with saffron

In Provence, this substantial dish traditionally graces the table at Easter

For this recipe, the broth is served as a first course with toasted bread, then the meat and vegetables are dished up on a warmed platter as a second course. The turnips (in French, *navets*) have a mild but characteristic flavor reminiscent of radishes. *Navets* are very popular in France and are available there year-round.

Quality poultry has its price: Bresse chickens, for example, are sold by an association of producers in eastern France under their own seal of quality. This guarantees stringent controls regarding feed, fattening age, and density in barns and runs. Poultry that is bred by the association is of consistently high quality and worth its premium price.

Serves 6

1 oven-ready chicken (about 3½ lb)
1¾ lb beef (bottom round or brisket)
10½ oz ham
1 medium onion, studded with 2 cloves and 1 bay leaf
¾ cup celery, cut into chunks; 5 crushed peppercorns
4 parsley sprigs, salt, 1 pinch saffron powder
You will also need:
8½ oz white turnips, cut into quarters or eighths
8½ oz baby carrots, with the green on top
1½ cups leeks, sliced ¾-inch thick
⅔ cup celery, sliced 1¼-inch thick

1. Wash the chicken thoroughly inside and out under cold water and let drain. Place the chicken, beef, and ham in a large pot with enough cold water to cover.

2. Add the studded onion, celery, peppercorns, and parsley sprigs. Season sparingly with salt, according to the saltiness of the ham.

3. Bring to a boil. Reduce heat and simmer for 1½–2 hours, repeatedly skimming off any scum that rises to the surface. Remove from heat.

4. Remove the beef, chicken, and ham and set aside. Strain the liquid through a fine-mesh sieve, pour it back into the pot, and sprinkle in the saffron powder. Return to low heat, add the turnips and baby carrots, and simmer for 10 minutes. Add the leeks and celery and simmer for another 8–10 minutes, then adjust the seasonings. Keep warm. Cut the beef into slices, divide the chicken into 8–10 pieces, and cut the ham into bite-sized chunks.

5. Return the beef, chicken, and ham to the pot to heat through. Ladle into soup plates with the vegetables and serve.

Lobster soup

Made from lobster shells — one of the most
exquisite soups ever tasted

Lobster cooking times are based on weight. For the
first 1¼ pounds, cook for 10–12 minutes; for the
second 1¼ pounds, a further 10 minutes; and for
each additional 1¼ pounds, just 5 minutes more.

Serves 4
2 live lobsters (about 1½ lb each)
4 teaspoons olive oil, 4 teaspoons cognac
5 teaspoons butter; ¼ cup shallots, sliced into rings
⅔ cup sliced white onion; 1 diced garlic clove
½ cup leeks, ⅔ cup carrots, ½ cup celery, all sliced
7 oz ripe tomatoes, cut into eighths; 1 clove
3 crushed juniper berries, 1 bay leaf
1 sprig each thyme and tarragon
1 tablespoon tomato paste
1 cup white wine, ½ cup Noilly Prat vermouth
4½ cups fish stock, 1 teaspoon flour
salt, freshly ground white pepper
You will also need:
2 oz thin noodles, about ⅛ inch wide
½ cup heavy cream
tarragon sprigs for garnishing

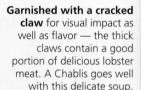

**Garnished with a cracked
claw** for visual impact as
well as flavor — the thick
claws contain a good
portion of delicious lobster
meat. A Chablis goes well
with this delicate soup.

1. Bring a large pot of water to a roiling boil, add
the lobsters headfirst and replace the lid. Make
sure that you add the second lobster only after the
water comes back to a boil. Reduce heat and
simmer for 20 minutes. Remove, rinse briefly in
ice water, and let cool.

2. Cut each lobster in half lengthwise along the
centerline, starting at the head. Remove the
stomach sac and intestines and discard. Take out
the coral (if present) and liver, and set aside.
Twist off each tail-half from the head, remove the
meat, and set aside. Twist off the claws and legs,
cracking them with a knife, and set aside.

3. Carefully wash the lobster shells (including
the legs) under cold water and let dry. Chop the
shells into small pieces. Heat the olive oil in a
pan and sauté the shells until lightly colored. Add
the cognac, simmer, remove from heat, and set
aside.

4. Melt the butter in a pot and sauté the shallots, onion, garlic, leeks, carrots, celery, and tomatoes. Add the herbs and spices and continue to sauté. Stir in the tomato paste and simmer for 2 minutes.

5. Add the reserved lobster shells to the pot. Pour in the wine and vermouth and simmer. Reduce the liquid over low heat until it is almost completely evaporated.

6. Pour in the fish stock and simmer for about 45 minutes, skimming off any scum that rises to the surface. Remove from heat, line a conical strainer with a double layer of cheesecloth, and strain in batches, pressing down hard to extract all the juices. Return to the pot. Stir the reserved liver and coral together with the flour until smooth and add to the soup. Bring to a boil, season with salt and pepper, and keep warm.

7. Cook the noodles until *al dente* and drain. Whip the cream until it forms soft peaks and fold into the soup. Cut the lobster meat into slices, add to the pot along with the claws, and slowly warm. Ladle into heated bowls with the noodles and garnish with a tarragon sprig.

Razor clam and vegetable soup

French chefs are famous for their imaginative use of shellfish

A court bouillon, cooked separately and containing a lavish amount of white wine, forms the basis of this soup. Additional flavor is imparted by a special bouquet garni for fish and seafood, composed of tarragon, thyme, parsley, celery, and lemon peel.

Serves 4
For the court bouillon:
2¼ cups white wine
1 cup carrots, ⅔ cup onion, ½ cup celery, ½ cup leeks; all coarsely chopped
2 garlic cloves, 1 bouquet garni (see below)
1 teaspoon sea salt, 5 black peppercorns
For the broth:
3 tablespoons olive oil, ⅔ cup finely chopped shallots, 1 finely chopped garlic clove
2 tablespoons tomato paste, 3¼ cups court bouillon (prepared separately)
2 thyme sprigs, 1 bay leaf, 2 tablespoons butter
1 pinch saffron powder
salt, freshly ground pepper
For the vegetable garnish:
2 tablespoons olive oil
½ cup thinly sliced celery; 1 cup yellow pepper, 4 oz zucchini, both cut into ½-inch chunks
7 oz beefsteak tomatoes, blanched, skinned, seeded, and diced

An aromatic scent wafts up from this soup made from the long, slender bivalves. Razor clams can be quite sandy and should be washed thoroughly before consuming.

salt, freshly ground pepper
For the shellfish:
1¾ lb razor clams, 1½ cups court bouillon (prepared separately)
You will also need:
2 tablespoons chopped herbs (parsley, tarragon, etc.)

1. To make the court bouillon, pour the wine and 2⅔ cups of water into a pot. Add the carrots, onion, celery, leeks, garlic, bouquet garni (1 sprig each of tarragon, thyme, and parsley; a little celeriac; a few celery leaves; and 1 piece of lemon peel), salt, and peppercorns. Bring to a boil. Reduce heat and simmer gently for 20 minutes.

Remove from heat and strain into a clean pot.

2. For the broth, heat the olive oil in a pot and sauté the shallots and garlic until translucent. Stir in the tomato paste, then pour in the court bouillon. Add the thyme sprigs and bay leaf, and simmer for 10 minutes over low heat. Add the butter, letting it melt; season with saffron powder, salt, and pepper. Keep the broth warm.

3. For the vegetable garnish, heat the olive oil in a pan and sauté the celery and pepper for 5 minutes, stirring occasionally. Add the zucchini and tomatoes and sauté for 5 minutes, then season with salt and pepper. Add the sautéed

vegetables to the broth and simmer for 3–4 minutes. Keep warm.

4. Place the razor clams in cold water for 10 minutes, then rinse well under cold water and let drain.

5. Bring the court bouillon to a boil. Add the clams, cover the pot, and simmer for 5 minutes over medium heat. Remove the clams with a slotted spoon, then strain the liquid through a fine-mesh sieve and add to the broth.

6. Ladle the broth, vegetables, and razor clams into soup plates; sprinkle with the chopped herbs.

Free-range chickens
are still the order of the
day on Scottish farms —
after all, one thing they
have quite a bit of there
is space!

Cock-a-leekie soup

A traditional dish from Scotland — chicken soup with leeks and prunes

This is a slight twist on the usual recipe for cock-a-leekie soup. A more filling variation can be made by adding cooked barley to the pot. If a plump, young chicken is used instead of a boiling fowl, choose one weighing about 3½ pounds and reduce the cooking time to 40 minutes.

Serves 4

1 dressed boiling fowl (about 4½ lb)
2 teaspoons salt, 1 small onion, halved
1 parsley stalk, 1 thyme sprig
1 mace flower, ½ teaspoon black peppercorns, 2 allspice berries, and 1 bay leaf tied in cheesecloth
1⅔ lb leeks, halved lengthwise and chopped
freshly ground white pepper and allspice

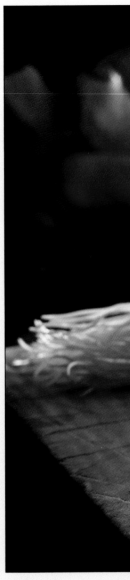

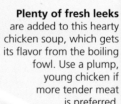

Plenty of fresh leeks
are added to this hearty
chicken soup, which gets
its flavor from the boiling
fowl. Use a plump,
young chicken if
more tender meat
is preferred.

You will also need:

12 pitted prunes

1. Wash the chicken thoroughly and pat dry with paper towels. Pour 9 cups of water in a large pot; add the chicken and season with salt.

2. Add the onion and bring to a boil. Reduce heat and add the herbs and spices to the pot. Add one-fourth of the leeks and simmer.

3. Skim off any scum that rises to the surface. Continue simmering over low heat for 1½ hours.

4. Remove from heat and take out the chicken; it should be fully cooked. Remove the skin, separate the meat from the bones, and slice into pieces. Set aside.

5. Strain the liquid through a fine-mesh sieve into a pot, then add the reserved leeks and bring to a boil. Reduce heat and simmer until the leeks are tender. Season to taste with pepper and allspice.

6. Add the sliced chicken and the prunes, heat, then remove from heat and allow the flavors to mingle for several minutes before serving.

Irish stew
Made with lamb or mutton — the culinary classic from the Emerald Isle

Irish stew, a typically Irish dish made of mutton or lamb, potatoes, onions, and thyme, is the most internationally famous stew from the British Isles. But this combination of ingredients is also extremely popular in England, known in Yorkshire and Lancashire as a "hot pot." Numerous variations of this hearty dish can be found throughout Great Britain and Ireland; in the version given here, the stew is also enriched with carrots, celery, and white cabbage. The ingredients are built up layer by layer in an ovenproof pot, the first and last layers consisting of potatoes. Everything is then braised slowly in liquid, in this case lamb stock. The resulting stew is as simple as it is delicious.

A black head is the hallmark of the aptly named Scottish blackface sheep — also raised extensively in Ireland — highly esteemed for the quality of its meat.

Serves 4
1¾ lb potatoes, sliced ⅛-inch thick
2¼ lb lamb from the leg bone, cut into 1-inch cubes
1 large onion, sliced into ⅛-inch rings; 1⅓ cup carrots, sliced ¼-inch thick
1¼ lb white cabbage, thinly sliced or shaved
⅔ cup thinly sliced celery
salt, freshly ground pepper
4 thyme sprigs
2 tablespoons chopped parsley
2¼ cups lamb stock
For the garnish:
chopped parsley

1. Preheat the oven to 315–325⁰. Layer the potatoes, lamb, onion, carrots, cabbage, and celery in a large ovenproof pot, sprinkling each layer with salt, pepper, thyme, and parsley. Finish off with a layer of potatoes.

2. Carefully pour in the lamb stock along one side of the pot. Cook for 1½–2 hours in the oven, periodically checking the level of the liquid and adding a little extra lamb stock if necessary. The topmost layer of potatoes should turn golden brown.

3. Remove from the oven, garnish with a little parsley, and serve.

Porcini mushrooms can be wormy, and if buying them at a farmer's market, make sure they are halved before purchase so their quality is assured.

Porcini soup

With smoked, raw ham — a first-rate soup redolent of late summer

In addition to the field mushroom, which grows in abundance in Belgian meadows, the coveted cèpe or porcini can also be found in the countryside from time to time. These mushrooms grow during spells of favorable weather, chiefly in the Soignes Forest and in the Ardennes, the hilly southern part of the country. *Ar Duenn* (the Gloom) has been the name for the mountain range with its marshes and moors, as far back as Celtic times. Heath and timber forest are also found there, though — just the right sort of place for a mushrooming expedition. Those who are not fortunate enough to be able to search for these fungi in such a lovely locale have the option of buying them fresh from the market.

This highly aromatic soup with its garnish of sautéed mushrooms and fried bread is a spicy delight. As fresh mushrooms come into season, this recipe is well worth trying.

Serves 4
5 tablespoons butter
½ cup finely chopped onion
5½ oz diced smoked, raw ham
10½ oz thinly sliced porcini mushrooms
6½ cups beef stock
salt, freshly ground pepper
freshly grated nutmeg
You will also need:
¼ cup butter
about 8 slices day-old white bread
3½ oz thinly sliced porcini mushrooms, salt
freshly ground pepper
1 tablespoon chopped parsley

1. Melt the butter in a pot and sauté the onion and ham for 2–3 minutes. Add the mushrooms and sauté briefly, stirring continuously. Pour in 2¼ cups of beef stock and bring to a boil. Reduce heat and simmer for 30–35 minutes, stirring occasionally.

2. Remove from heat and strain the contents of the pot through a fine-mesh sieve into a bowl. Heat the remaining beef stock and add back the strained porcini purée. Season with salt, pepper, and nutmeg. Simmer over low heat for 15 minutes, adding a little more beef stock if necessary. Keep warm.

3. Melt 7½ teaspoons of butter in a frying pan and fry the bread slices on both sides until golden brown. Remove and transfer to warmed soup plates.

4. Heat the remaining butter and fry the mushrooms for 1–2 minutes. Season lightly with salt and pepper.

5. Ladle the soup over the fried bread slices, divide the sautéed mushrooms among the soup plates, sprinkle with parsley, and serve.

Pigeon pot-au-feu

A highlight of Belgian culinary art — first browned, then poached, the birds are especially succulent

With a classic, French-style pot-au-feu, the meat and poultry are boiled together in a pot — the emphasis being on the word "boiled." In this recipe, by contrast, the pigeon pieces are first sautéed in olive oil, which gives them their appetizing color, and then are added to the soup.

Serves 4
2 oven-ready pigeons (about 8½ oz each)
salt, freshly ground white pepper
½ cup red lentils, 5 tablespoons olive oil
¾ cup finely chopped onion
1 finely chopped garlic clove
¾ cup thinly sliced celery
¾ cup leeks, sliced into ⅛-inch rings; ½ cup carrots, diced into ¼-inch cubes
3½ oz baby turnips, cut into quarters or eighths (depending on size)
3¼ cups light chicken stock
1 bay leaf
1 thyme sprig
For the garnish:
a few parsley leaves

1. Wash the pigeons inside and out under cold water, then carefully pat dry. Halve the birds, cutting off the legs. Season with salt and pepper, and refrigerate.

2. Pour the lentils into a sieve or colander, rinse thoroughly under cold water, and drain. Heat 1 tablespoon of olive oil in a pot, add one-third of the onion, and sauté briefly. Stir in the lentils, pour in 1⅛ cups of water, and bring to a boil. Reduce heat and simmer for 10 minutes, until almost cooked. Remove from heat and set aside.

3. In the meantime, heat the remaining olive oil in a stew pan, add the pigeon pieces, and brown on all sides. Remove the pigeon pieces and set aside. Sauté the rest of the onion and the garlic until translucent. Add the celery, leeks, carrots, and baby turnips and sauté briefly.

4. Add the browned pigeon pieces back to the pan, pour in the chicken stock, and bring to a boil. Reduce heat and simmer for 20 minutes. Add 1 teaspoon of salt, the bay leaf, thyme, and the partially cooked lentils, then season with pepper and simmer for another 5 minutes, until the pigeon and the vegetables are tender.

5. Ladle the soup into heated bowls, dividing the pigeon pieces evenly, and garnish with a little parsley. Serve immediately.

Worteltje soup with smoked-fish mousse

This recipe proves that an excellent carrot soup can be created from simple ingredients

The colonial Southeast Asia Dutch continued to use exotic spices on their return home. The spiciness of fresh ginger in this soup gives the mild carrot a kick.

Serves 4
For the smoked-fish mousse:
¾ cup fish stock
4 oz smoked trout fillet, skinned and cut into small chunks (reserve the skin)
7 teaspoons diced shallots, 1 diced garlic clove
1 teaspoon cornstarch dissolved in a little water
½ teaspoon gelatin dissolved in cold water
¾ cup heavy cream
salt, freshly ground pepper
For the carrot soup:
1¾ lb carrots, 10 teaspoons butter
1¼ cups diced onion, ½ oz diced ginger
4½ cups vegetable stock
salt, freshly ground pepper, sugar

Carrots galore: This soup, exotically spiced with ginger and full of vitamins as well, tastes best made from freshly picked, early summer carrots.

A soupçon (trace) of chervil rounds out the flavor of this choicely garnished soup, the splash of green creating an eye-catching contrast to the bright orange background.

For the garnish:

chervil leaves

1. To make the mousse, bring the fish stock to a boil. Add the trout skin, shallots, and garlic and simmer for 10 minutes. Remove the trout skin.

2. Add the cornstarch and thicken slightly. Stir in the trout pieces and simmer for 5 minutes. Remove from heat. Blend until smooth and pour into a bowl. Add the gelatin to the still-warm liquid. Whip the cream until it forms soft peaks. As the mousse begins to set, fold in the cream, season to taste, and refrigerate overnight.

3. The next day, set aside about 1¼ carrots and finely dice the remainder. Heat the butter in a large pot and sauté the diced carrots, onion, and ginger. Pour in 3¾ cups of vegetable stock and bring to a boil. Reduce heat and simmer, covered, for 30 minutes. Remove from heat and purée until smooth. Season with salt, pepper, and sugar.

4. Cook the reserved carrots in the remaining vegetable stock for 5 minutes; add to the soup.

5. Ladle into soup plates. Mold the chilled mousse into little dumplings, and drop into the soup. Garnish with chervil and serve immediately.

Two-tone vegetable soup

A delight for both the palate and the eye; soup cuisine doesn't get much more colorful than this

In the land of vegetable growing par excellence, fresh vegetables naturally have an important role in cooking. And it is precisely as soup that carrots, zucchini, and so on find a delicious expression, time after time. Here, the appropriate seasoning is what matters most. The delight of this two-part dish is the contrast between the fruity-hot carrot soup and the creamy zucchini soup.

Serves 4

For the carrot soup:
¼ cup butter, ⅓ cup diced white onion
1½ teaspoons diced ginger, 4½ cups diced carrots
½ red chile pepper, finely chopped
4½ cups vegetable stock
4½ teaspoons heavy cream blended with dash of buttermilk (crème fraîche)
juice of 2 oranges
salt, freshly ground white pepper
For the zucchini soup:
½ oz dried porcini mushrooms, 10½ oz zucchini
¼ cup butter, ⅓ cup chopped shallots, 8½ oz cubed mealy potatoes, 3¾ cups vegetable stock
salt, freshly ground pepper
10 teaspoons cream (optional)
For the garnish:
nasturtium flowers

1. To make the carrot (yellow) soup, melt the butter in a large pot and sauté the onion and ginger without letting them brown. Add the carrots and chile pepper and sauté for another 3–4 minutes. Pour in the vegetable stock and bring to a boil. Reduce heat and simmer for 20 minutes. Remove from heat and blend until smooth. Fold in the crème fraîche and orange juice, and season with salt and pepper. Reheat before serving.

2. To make the zucchini (green) soup, soak the mushrooms in lukewarm water for 30 minutes. Remove and drain, squeeze out the excess moisture, and finely chop. Set aside. Strain the soaking water through a fine-mesh sieve and set aside also.

3. Cut off both ends of the zucchini and peel, taking care to save the peel. Finely chop this and set aside. Dice the zucchini and set aside.

4. Melt the butter in a pot and sauté the shallots and mushrooms without letting them brown. Add the diced zucchini and potatoes and sauté for 3–4 minutes. Pour in the vegetable stock and the strained, mushroom-soaking liquid and bring to a boil. Reduce heat and simmer for 15 minutes; add the zucchini peel during the final 3–4 minutes. Remove from heat and blend until smooth. Pour the soup back into the pot, reheat, season with salt and pepper, and add the cream if desired. Ladle the two soups decoratively into soup plates, garnish with nasturtium flowers, and serve.

White cabbage.
Cabbage has always played an important role in Danish cooking. It is often seasoned with caraway seeds, as in this recipe.

Vegetable stew with pickled pork

Slice and dice the meat and vegetables, layer in a pot, toss it into the oven, and dinner's made

Contrary to popular opinion, Danish cooking is by no means restricted to fish. A flat country with a long coastline, Denmark has a well-developed agricultural industry, with dairy farming and pig breeding as two important cornerstones. It's not a surprise then that the Danes have a predilection for pork in all its forms, whether roasted with a brown crust or made into *frikadeller* (meatballs). Also popular, however, are the substantial and hearty pickled-pork stews, since it is precisely the simple things that Danes appreciate most. These stews also contain an assortment of vegetables. Because the climate is relatively cool, hardy varieties such as leeks, beets, and celeriac play an important role, as well as cabbage and potatoes, which are essential to this and other dishes. A Danish dessert, such as a slice of apple cake or pancakes hot out of the pan — both served with healthy spoonfuls of cream — makes a thoroughly delicious if self-indulgent end to the meal. *Velbekomme* ("Enjoy"), as they say in Denmark!

Serves 4

2¼ lb white cabbage, cut into thin strips
2¼ lb pickled pork (from the shoulder), cut into ¾-inch cubes
2½ cups finely chopped onion
3 finely chopped garlic cloves
2¾ cups carrots, cut into ½-inch pieces
1¾ lb potatoes, cut into ¾-inch chunks
3 tablespoons chopped parsley
½ teaspoon caraway seeds
salt, freshly ground black pepper
3½ cups vegetable stock

1. Preheat the oven to 350⁰. Layer the cabbage in an ovenproof pot. On top of the cabbage, layer the pork, onion, garlic, carrots, potatoes, and parsley, then sprinkle with caraway seeds and season with salt and pepper.

2. Heat the vegetable stock in a second pot, and pour over the layered meat and vegetables. Cover the ovenproof pot and bake for about 90 minutes. Adjust the seasonings and serve.

This tasty stew containing white cabbage, potatoes, and pickled pork is both simple and hearty. The Danes know how to make a lot from a little, and meat — preferably pork — and potatoes are usually part of the equation.

The Town Hall of Copenhagen, an emblem of this city of many towers that was founded around 1160 — famous not only for the Tivoli Gardens but also for its fine cuisine.

Gulerod soup

Coconut milk and curry powder lend an Asian touch to this excellent carrot soup

Copenhagen — not only the city of the "Little Mermaid" that has had to endure major incursions from its neighbors on a regular basis — is also a city of tempting food displays and numerous cafés, bars, and restaurants. Once there, the ubiquitous but delicious *smørrebrød* (buttered, open-faced sandwich) is encountered at almost every turn; but soups also play an important role here, as they do throughout Denmark and indeed all of Scandinavia. The Danes love their soups seasoned in various ways and sumptuous — at least as far as butter and cream are concerned. Thus, a splash of heavy cream is essential in this delicious vegetable soup made from baby carrots — but only as a garnish, snaking decoratively across the top. The soup derives its exquisite, exotic flavor primarily from the unsweetened coconut milk folded into the puréed carrots, as well as curry powder, which completes the Far Eastern note.

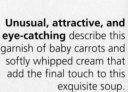

Unusual, attractive, and eye-catching describe this garnish of baby carrots and softly whipped cream that add the final touch to this exquisite soup.

Tender young carrots, freshly picked, are the best foundation for this soup and garnish. Naturally, they taste best fresh from one's own garden.

Serves 4
1 tablespoon vegetable oil
½ cup coarsely chopped scallions
4½ cups diced carrots
1 tablespoon curry powder
3½ cups chicken stock
1½ cups unsweetened coconut milk
salt, freshly ground white pepper
pinch cayenne pepper
lemon juice
For the garnish:
12 trimmed baby carrots, with green tufts left on
⅓ cup heavy cream
parsley leaves

1. Heat the vegetable oil in a pot and sauté the scallions until lightly browned. Add the carrots and sauté for 3–4 minutes, then stir in the curry powder. Pour in the chicken stock and bring to a boil. Reduce heat and simmer, covered, for about 25 minutes.

2. Blend the contents of the pot to a fine purée with a handheld blender. Stir the coconut milk in a small bowl until smooth, then fold into the soup. Season with salt, pepper, cayenne pepper, and lemon juice, then simmer for another 2–3 minutes. Keep warm.

3. Cook the baby carrots in boiling, salted water for 10–12 minutes. Remove, drain well, and set aside.

4. Whip the cream until it forms soft peaks. Ladle the hot soup into warmed bowls. Spoon the cream into a piping bag with a round tip and pipe a wavy line over each bowl. Garnish with the baby carrots and parsley leaves, and serve immediately.

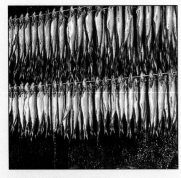

Herring, hanging in neat and tidy rows. The herring of the Baltic island of Bornholm is reputed to be a special delicacy when freshly smoked. If it is to be used as a garnish for this pea soup, plan on using about 8½ oz total.

Pea soup

A specialty soup popular throughout Scandinavia — especially tasty when made with fresh green peas

In Scandinavia, pea soups are prepared from yellow or green split peas, depending on the region. This recipe, however, uses fresh peas cooked in veal stock and then puréed for a pleasant, fresh vegetable flavor. This pea soup can either be served plain, garnished with a few croutons and fresh mint leaves, or else with a delicate, smoked-fish accompaniment, for which a wide variety — from herring to salmon — can be used.

Serves 4
For the croutons:
7½ teaspoons butter
2–3 slices white bread (crusts removed), cut into ¼-inch cubes
For the soup:
1⅓ lb freshly shelled peas (about 3¼ lb in their pods)
salt, 10 teaspoons butter
¾ cup finely chopped onion
1 finely chopped garlic clove
3¾ cups veal stock
freshly ground pepper
pinch freshly grated nutmeg
½ cup heavy cream

For the garnish:
1 tablespoon chopped mint

1. First prepare the croutons: Melt the butter in a frying pan and fry the bread cubes, stirring, until golden brown. Remove and set aside.

2. Simmer about one-sixth of the peas in lightly boiling, salted water for 5 minutes. Drain, rinse under cold water, and set aside.

3. Melt the butter in a pot and sauté the onion and garlic until translucent. Add the uncooked peas and sauté for 5 minutes. Pour in the veal stock. Season with salt, pepper, and nutmeg. Simmer over low heat for 10 minutes.

4. Remove from heat, purée the contents of the pot with a handheld blender until smooth, and strain through a fine-mesh sieve into a pot or soup tureen. Whip the cream until it forms soft peaks and carefully fold into the tureen. Mix in the blanched peas and adjust the seasonings.

5. Ladle the soup into warmed bowls and top with the croutons. Garnish with a little chopped mint if desired, and serve immediately while still hot.

Shelling the peas is tedious work, but worth the trouble. This exquisite pea soup is rounded out with a little whipped cream, blanched peas, and croutons.

Fish soup

Based on a homemade stock made from fish bones and root vegetables

Fresh fish has an even greater role in the cuisine of Norway than in that of its Scandinavian neighbors — especially cod, which, when not dried and salted, is almost always boiled.

Serves 4
For the fish stock:
3 lb gutted haddock or codfish
2 tablespoons vegetable oil
½ cup shallots, ¾ cup leeks (white part only), ½ cup parsley root, ⅓ cup celery, all diced
1⅛ cups white wine
1 bay leaf, 10 white peppercorns
For the soup:
10 teaspoons butter
1 small onion, halved and sliced into half-moons
1 teaspoon curry powder, 1¾ lb potatoes, diced into ½-inch cubes
salt, freshly ground white pepper
¾ cup leeks; 1 cup carrots, both cut into julienne strips
For the garnish:
1 tablespoon chopped dill

The choicest fish soup: There are many variations of this Norwegian national dish — each family has its own special recipe, some with sour cream, some with egg yolks. Here, a delicate, clear version is presented with chunks of fish fillet (simmered only briefly) and fresh dill.

Lone farmhouses scattered across the immense Norwegian landscape are usually very cozy inside. This is hardly surprising, since the most important room in the house is, and always has been, the kitchen.

1. Cut the heads off the fish. Grip each tail and cut off the fins in the direction of the head. Scrape off the scales, also working from the tail toward the head. Wash the fish carefully inside and out under cold water. Fillet the bodies and refrigerate.

2. Remove the gills from the head and discard. Rinse the fish bones and heads under cold water or until the water runs off clear. Drain well.

3. For the fish stock, heat the vegetable oil in a large pot and sauté the fish bones, heads, tails,

and trimmings for 4 minutes, stirring constantly, until slightly browned. Add the shallots, leeks, parsley root, and celery and sauté over low heat, stirring frequently. As soon as the mixture simmers, pour in the wine and reduce slightly. Add 5¼ cups of water, the bay leaf, and the peppercorns. Bring to a boil, skimming off any scum that rises to the surface. Simmer for 20 minutes. Remove from heat, line a conical strainer with cheesecloth, and pour the stock through freely into a pot.

4. For the soup, melt the butter in a pot and sauté the onion until translucent. Sprinkle in the curry powder and pour in the prepared fish stock. Add the potatoes and simmer for 10 minutes, then season with salt and pepper. Add the leeks and carrots and simmer for another 5 minutes.

5. Cut the fish fillets into ¾-inch pieces, add to the soup, and simmer for 3–4 minutes. Adjust the seasonings, garnish with a little chopped dill, and serve.

Like other fresh vegetables, asparagus is relatively expensive in Norway, since it usually must be imported. Nonetheless, it is such a wonderful partner for the delicate-tasting salmon that you should indulge anyway — especially if it is more affordable where you live.

Salmon dumpling soup

Salmon goes with Norway like ham with eggs, which explains why this mouth-watering fish is almost always on the menu there

The variety of salmon from clear mountain streams is regarded as being of the best quality. Here is a delicate recipe, in which the salmon is featured in the soup both as quenelles (dumplings) and as chunks of fillet.

Serves 4
For the salmon dumplings:
8½ oz well-chilled salmon fillet, cut into cubes
salt, freshly ground white pepper
1 cup well-chilled heavy cream
For the soup:
5¼ cups fish stock
8 teaspoons shallots, 1 garlic clove
½ cup celery, ⅔ cup leeks, all thinly sliced
7 oz white asparagus, cut into 1½-inch pieces
7 oz tomatoes, blanched, peeled, seeded, and diced into ¼-inch cubes
1 bay leaf, 1 thyme sprig
salt, freshly ground pepper
7 oz salmon fillet, cut into ½-inch cubes
1 teaspoon lemon juice, 1 teaspoon chopped celery leaves
pinch cayenne pepper, zest of ½ lemon
For the garnish:
1 tablespoon chopped parsley, a few thyme leaves

1. First, prepare the dumpling mixture: Season the salmon cubes with salt and pepper, and put through the finest blade of a meat grinder or mix in a food processor. Transfer the mixture to a bowl that has been placed in a larger bowl filled with ice cubes. Add about ⅓ cup of cream to the bowl and mix well. Purée the mixture in batches, but for no longer than absolutely necessary — it must not get too warm. Press the mixture through a fine-mesh sieve into a bowl, in order to remove any residual bone matter. Stir in about ⅓ cup of cream until the mixture is smooth. Whip the remaining cream lightly and fold into the dumpling mixture. Adjust the seasonings and refrigerate.

2. For the soup, heat the fish stock in a large pot. Add the shallots, garlic, celery, leeks, asparagus, and tomatoes, together with the bay leaf and thyme sprig. Season with salt and pepper and simmer for 5 minutes. Keep warm.

3. To form the dumplings, dip two tablespoons in cold water, then use to shape oval dumplings from the salmon mixture. Slide the dumplings into the hot soup and simmer over low heat for 8 minutes, or until done.

4. Add the cubed salmon fillet to the soup during the last 3–4 minutes of cooking time. Season with lemon juice, celery leaves, and cayenne pepper. Sprinkle in the lemon zest. Ladle into warmed soup plates and serve garnished with parsley and thyme.

Polski Barszcz

Borscht, Polish style, with specially brewed kvass (soured beets) and Polish sausage

Several Eastern European countries, among them Russia, Romania, and Poland, claim to be the source of this popular stew containing beets and sour cream, of which there are at least 100 different variations. For this Polish version, a special kvass made only of beets and water serves as the soup base; kvass for drinking is usually made with brewer's yeast.

Serves 4
For the kvass:
2¼ lb coarsely shredded beets
For the stock:
9 cups kvass (prepared separately), 1¼ lb beef (bottom round)
⅔ cup onion, cut into chunks; ¾ cup celeriac, cut into chunks
1 cup carrots, cut into chunks; ½ cup leeks, cut into chunks
1 oz dried mushrooms
8½ oz uncooked, smoked pork belly
For the borscht:
¼ cup butter, ⅔ cup finely chopped onion
1⅓ lb beets, thinly sliced and chopped into very thin sticks
3 tablespoons flour, 4 small thinly sliced Polish sausages
salt, freshly ground pepper
mild wine vinegar

Unusually colored, but delicious. This beet stew is good on cold days served piping hot, but can also be served chilled in the summer. In both cases, sour cream is just the right accompaniment.

½ cup sour cream
For the garnish:
1 tablespoon chopped dill

1. To make the kvass, place the shredded beets in a stoneware pot with just enough cold water to cover. Set a plate on top of the beets and weigh down. Leave, uncovered, in a cool, dark place for 8 days. After that time, strain the beets, carefully pressing down to squeeze out the slightly sour liquid — there should be about 9 cups. Discard the beets.

2. To make the stock, pour the kvass into a large pot with the beef. Add the onion, celeriac, carrots, and leeks and bring to a boil. Reduce heat and simmer for 30 minutes. Add the mushrooms and pork belly, and simmer for another hour over low heat. Remove the beef, pork belly, and mushrooms, and set aside. Strain the stock through a fine-mesh sieve into a bowl and set aside.

3. For the borscht, melt the butter in a large pot and sauté the onion until lightly browned. Add

the beets and sauté briefly; sprinkle in the flour and simmer, stirring, for 2–3 minutes. Pour in the prepared stock, bring to a boil, and simmer over low heat for 10–15 minutes.

4. Cut the beef and the pork belly into ½-inch cubes. Finely dice the reserved mushrooms; add them, the beef, pork belly, and sausage to the borscht and simmer for 10 minutes. Season with salt, pepper, and vinegar. Remove from heat and stir in the sour cream. Garnish with dill and serve with a fresh loaf of bread.

Sauerkraut-cream soup with blood sausage dumplings

A specialty of Bohemian soup cuisine that features well-seasoned, smoked, blood sausage

Serves 4

2 tablespoons vegetable oil
2–3 slices uncooked bacon, 4 juniper berries
⅔ cup finely chopped onion, 1 finely chopped garlic clove
½ cup finely chopped celeriac
4½ cups veal stock, 1½ cups sauerkraut
1 bay leaf, 5½ oz potatoes, cut into cubes; 1¼ cups cream
salt, freshly ground pepper
For the blood sausage dumplings:
3½ oz smoked blood sausage, skinned and finely diced
¼ cup finely chopped shallots
3½ oz ground meat (half pork and half beef)
1 teaspoon chopped marjoram
1 teaspoon chopped parsley, 1 egg yolk
salt, freshly ground pepper
For the batter:
¾ cup flour, ⅓ cup pale ale, 1 egg yolk, salt, 1 egg white
You will also need:
vegetable oil for deep-frying
5 teaspoons cold butter, in pieces

1. Heat the oil and brown the bacon and juniper berries. Add the onion, garlic, and celeriac and sauté briefly. Add the veal stock and simmer. Lightly squeeze out the sauerkraut, reserving the juices; set aside ¼ cup. Add the remaining sauerkraut, bay leaf, and potatoes, and simmer for 40 minutes. Stir in the cream, simmer for another 20 minutes. Season with salt and pepper; remove from heat.

2. To make the dumplings, add together all the ingredients and knead well. Form the mixture into 8 small dumplings.

3. To make the batter, sift the flour into a bowl and stir in the beer until smooth. Blend in the egg yolk and season with salt. Whip the egg white until it forms stiff peaks and fold into the batter.

4. Heat the vegetable oil to 300⁰. Dip the dumplings into the batter, shake off any excess, and fry for 4 minutes, until light brown. Remove and drain on paper towels. Fry the reserved sauerkraut in a sieve in the hot oil until crispy. Remove and drain on paper towels

5. Remove the bacon and juniper berries from the soup and discard. Purée until very smooth and pour through a sieve. Re-heat and season with sauerkraut juice, salt, and pepper. Add the butter and blend until foamy. Ladle into bowls, garnish with the crisp-fried sauerkraut, and serve.

Crisp-fried sauerkraut makes an interesting complement for this mellow soup with its delicate, blood sausage dumplings.

Vegetable soup with groats

Groat soup has been known since the Middle Ages and can be prepared with various ingredients — here, with mushrooms

Originally a poor man's dish — especially in places where it was made with just water — groat soup has gradually come up in the world. Over time, its image has improved considerably with the addition of stock and butter, and even bacon or some other meat. Somewhere along the line, though, groats once again fell into relative neglect as a soup ingredient, and were consigned to food for convalescents. Today, it is well worth it to become reacquainted with the culinary uses of this grain product — here, the hulled, peeled, round-milled, polished barley or wheat grains whose special hallmark is their light color (a result of the milling process). The most delicate member of the family is so-called pearl barley: particularly small, round grains such as those used in this soup, whose flavor is rounded out by

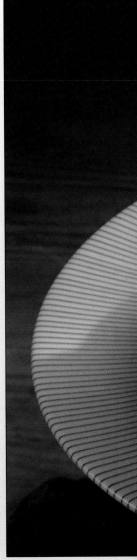

Fresh mushrooms, ideally picked in the wild, give this rustic, hearty soup its special flavor.

smoked bacon and fresh mushrooms. If pearl barley is unavailable though, any barley will substitute nicely.

Serves 4
½ cup pearl barley, salt
⅓ cup diced, uncooked, smoked bacon
⅔ cup finely diced white onion
½ cup finely diced carrots
½ cup finely diced parsley root
½ cup finely diced leeks

4½–5¼ cups vegetable stock
salt, freshly ground black pepper
1 tablespoon chopped parsley
5 teaspoons butter, 7 oz thinly sliced fresh mushrooms

1. Thoroughly wash the barley and soak overnight in water. The next day, drain and place the barley in a pot with enough fresh water to cover. Salt lightly and cook for 15 minutes over low heat, then drain and set aside.

2. Cook the bacon in a pot until the fat can be swirled around. Add the onion and sauté without letting it brown. Add the carrots, parsley root, and leeks and sauté for 3–4 minutes. Pour in the vegetable stock and bring to a boil. Reduce heat, add the pearl barley, and simmer for about 30 minutes until soft. Season with salt and pepper, and sprinkle in the parsley. Keep warm.

3. Melt the butter in a frying pan and briefly fry the mushrooms. Season sparingly with salt and pepper.

4. Add the mushrooms to the soup and simmer for 2–3 minutes. Ladle into heated soup plates or bowls and serve.

Chilled elderberry soup

The aromatic berries are transformed with apples, red wine, and spices into a refreshing, cold delicacy

In the fall, juicy, black berries develop from spicy-scented blossoms on the parasol-shaped clusters of the elder bush. October is the best month for picking, but it is likely the birds, who are very partial to the fruit, will get there first. Elderberries are inedible in their raw state, as they contain a substance that breaks down into prussic acid (a poison). Once cooked, however, the berries are extremely versatile and can be made into compote, purée, jelly, juice, or syrup; they also blend well with fruits such as oranges, damsons (Asian plums), pears, quinces, and rowanberries. In this recipe, the elderberries, which should be fully ripe, are combined with apples.

Serves 4

2¼ lb elderberries, with their stalks
1¼ cup red wine
1 cup sugar
peel of ½ lemon

1 small cinnamon stick, 2 whole cloves
3 small apples, peeled, cored, and sliced into thin wedges
¼ teaspoon cornstarch
Optional:
¼ cup heavy cream blended with ¼ teaspoon buttermilk (crème fraîche)

1. Wash the elderberries under cold water and drain well. Place the berries in the freezer until just frozen since the delicate fruit is easier to remove this way. Carefully strip the berries from their stalks by hand, taking care not to crush them. Set aside.

2. Bring the wine to a boil with the sugar, lemon peel, cinnamon stick, and cloves.

3. Add the elderberries and return to a boil, stirring frequently. Fold in the apple slices. Simmer for 15 minutes, repeatedly skimming off any foam that rises to the top. Dissolve the cornstarch in a little red wine and use to thicken the mixture. Refrigerate until serving time, adding in the crème fraîche (if desired) right before.

This autumn soup can be enriched with a little crème fraîche (heavy cream and buttermilk), if desired. It can also be prepared with 8½ oz of pears and 7 oz of apples for an extra fruity flavor.

White asparagus, which grows well on light, warm soils, is always harvested by hand, before the tips poke through to the sunlight. For this reason, this vegetable is still a fairly expensive luxury.

Chicken soup with asparagus
Creamy, yet light and spicy — an ideal springtime pairing

A homemade chicken stock forms the basis of this delicate cream soup. This recipe makes almost 3½ qt of stock. Just one-third is used for the soup; the remainder can be frozen.

Serves 4
1 prepared boiling chicken (about 4½ lb)
2¼ lb veal bones, cut into sections
2 crushed garlic cloves, 20 peppercorns
1 onion, studded with 4 cloves
bouquet garni (see below)
1¼ lb white asparagus, stalks only
10 teaspoons butter, 10 teaspoons flour
salt, freshly ground white pepper
dash lemon juice, ½ cup cream, 1 egg yolk
For the bouquet garni:
1 cup carrots, ⅔ cup leeks, ½ cup celery, all chopped
2 bay leaves, 2 thyme sprigs, 6 parsley stalks
For the garnish:
1 tablespoon diced chives

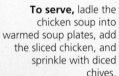

To serve, ladle the chicken soup into warmed soup plates, add the sliced chicken, and sprinkle with diced chives.

1. Wash the chicken under cold water; drain well, and cut into quarters. Place the chicken pieces and veal bones in a stockpot with enough hot water to cover and bring to a boil as quickly as possible.

Allow the liquid to well up until the protein and impurities rise to the surface. Pour off the water, and rinse the chicken and the veal bones with warm water. Return to the pot, cover with 4½ qt of fresh water, and return to a boil, skimming repeatedly. Reduce heat and keep at just under boiling for about 3 hours. After 2 hours, add the garlic, peppercorns, the clove-studded onion, and the bouquet garni. If necessary, add more water so that the chicken and veal bones remain covered.

2. Remove from heat and take out the chicken and bones, setting both aside. Remove the onion and strain the stock through a piece of cheesecloth into a pot; let cool, and skim off the fat. Measure off 4½ cups.

3. Bring the reserved stock to a boil; add the asparagus and simmer for 12–15 minutes. Remove from heat. Remove the asparagus with a slotted spoon, cut off 1½ inches from the tips, and set aside for the garnish. Purée the rest of the stalks in a blender until smooth. Set aside.

4. Melt the butter in a pot, add the flour, and sauté, stirring frequently, for 1–2 minutes without letting the flour brown. Pour in the stock, stir until smooth, and season with salt, pepper, and lemon juice. Stir in the cream and the asparagus purée. Simmer for about 20 minutes, stirring constantly.

5. Remove from heat and strain through a fine-mesh sieve. Return to low heat. Draw off a small amount of soup and stir the egg yolk into it, then use this to thicken the soup, taking care not to let it boil. Add the asparagus tips and keep hot.

6. Skin the chicken, separate the meat from the veal bones, and cut into bite-sized chunks or slices. Add back to the soup and top with diced chives right before serving.

Pichelsteiner

This mixed-meat and vegetable stew has become well known far beyond its native Germany

Two communities in the Bavarian forest, Regen and Grattersdorf, each claim to be the original home of this traditional dish, and compete every summer in a big festival in its honor. Pichelsteiner or "Büchelstoana" takes a lot of time and effort to prepare, so it is advisable to make it in larger quantities than required for just one meal. Any leftovers can be frozen and enjoyed later. Fresh-made bread and a well-chilled beer should be served with this hearty stew.

Serves 4

3½ oz beef marrow, removed from the bone
3¼ cups well-seasoned beef broth
8 tablespoons vegetable oil
8½ oz lamb (leg cut), cut into ½-inch cubes
8½ oz veal (shoulder cut), cut into ½-inch cubes
8½ oz pork (leg cut), cut into ½-inch cubes
8½ oz beef brisket, cut into ½-inch cubes
1¼ cups coarsely chopped onion
3 tablespoons chopped parsley
salt, freshly ground pepper
1⅓ cups carrots, cut into ½-inch pieces
1⅓ cups celeriac, cut into ½-inch pieces
7 oz potatoes, cut into ½-inch pieces
½ cup parsley root, cut into ½-inch pieces
1⅓ cups leeks, cut into ½-inch pieces
7 oz white cabbage (leaves), sliced into ¾-inch squares

Soak the beef marrow under cold water for about 15 minutes; it will turn completely white during this time. Clean the soaked marrow, cut into thin rounds, and set aside. Heat the beef broth in a pot and the vegetable oil in a large pan. Preheat the oven to 390–400⁰. Proceed as shown in the picture sequence opposite. Cover the ovenproof pot and cook the stew for about 90 minutes.

Combine all the different meats and sear in batches on all sides in hot oil. Add the onion and sauté briefly.

Place half of the marrow slices in an ovenproof pot and melt slightly over a low heat.

Next, spoon a layer of the meat and onion mixture on top of the marrow. Sprinkle with a little parsley, and season lightly with salt and pepper.

Top with a layer of vegetables. Continue to fill with alternating layers of meat and vegetables, sprinkling with parsley and seasoning with salt and pepper.

Finish with a layer of vegetables. Arrange the rest of the marrow on top and scatter over the remaining parsley. Pour in the hot broth.

Baltic Coast eel soup

A variant of the northern German classic, with bacon, vegetables, and croutons

It is easiest to buy the eel already skinned. If you prefer to remove the skin yourself, it is best to do it as shown in the picture sequence.

Serves 4
1 gutted eel (about 1¼ lb)
For the stock:
1 tablespoon vegetable oil
⅔ cup vegetables (onions, carrots, leeks, celery), all chopped into small pieces
½ cup white wine
2 whole cloves, 2 bay leaves
2 allspice berries, 5 peppercorns
For the soup:
7½ teaspoons butter
⅓ cup uncooked bacon, cut into small pieces
⅔ cup onion, halved and sliced into half-moons; 2 tablespoons flour
1 cup carrots, ⅔ cup celeriac, both cut into thin sticks; ⅔ cup leeks, sliced
salt, freshly ground pepper, dash lemon juice
¼ cup heavy cream blended with ¼ teaspoon buttermilk (crème fraîche)
2 tablespoons chopped dill
For the croutons:
7½ teaspoons butter
2–3 slices white bread (crusts removed), cut into ¼-inch cubes

Fillet the eel, cut it into ¾-inch-thick chunks, and refrigerate. To make the stock, chop the eel bones and skin. Rinse the bones and trimmings for 10 minutes. Remove and drain. Heat the vegetable oil and sauté the bones and trimmings for 3

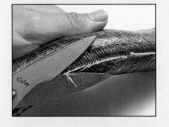

Skinning the eel: Loosen a flap of skin on one side behind the head. Ease your thumb along below the skin, loosening it all the way to the other side. Using this "handle," first pull the skin toward you over the head. Now grip the loose end of the skin with a cloth, and pull it back and off over the tail. Using scissors, cut off the fins in the direction of the head.

minutes, until lightly browned. Add the vegetables and sauté briefly, stirring frequently. Add the wine and simmer, reducing the liquid a little. Pour in 4 cups of water; add the herbs and spices and bring to a boil. Reduce heat and simmer for 20 minutes, repeatedly skimming off any scum that rises to the surface. Remove from heat, line a conical sieve with cheesecloth, strain the stock, and set aside. To make the soup, melt the butter in a pot and sauté the bacon and onion until translucent. Sprinkle in the flour, stir well, and continue sautéing without allowing the flour to brown. Pour in the prepared stock and simmer for 20 minutes; then add the carrots, celeriac, and leeks and simmer for another 10 minutes. Reduce heat, add the eel chunks, and simmer for 10 more minutes. Keep warm. Meanwhile, make the croutons: Melt the butter in a frying pan and sauté the bread cubes until golden brown. Season the soup with salt, pepper, and lemon juice; stir in the crème fraîche; and sprinkle with the chopped dill. Ladle into heated soup plates, sprinkle the croutons on top, and serve at once while they are still crisp.

Blanched asparagus grows in light, sandy soils in earth mounds that are built up at the beginning of spring. During the season — in Europe, from the beginning of May to the 24th of June — it is cut twice daily, before exposure to sunlight causes it to discolor. The surface of the soil is then smoothed flat again with a trowel.

Asparagus soup with crayfish tails

A garnish of choice crayfish transforms this appetizer into a true delicacy

The signal crayfish used in this recipe owe their name to the little splotch of orange on their claw joints. The shell coloring ranges from black to reddish green, with a light-brown underbelly. Originally native to the high-altitude mountain lakes of North America, these crayfish have also been released elsewhere in the world.

Serves 4
12 live crayfish (3 oz each), salt
1⅓ lb white asparagus
⅝ cup cream, 2 egg yolks
freshly ground white pepper
freshly grated nutmeg
You will also need:
½ cup cooked long-grain rice
chervil leaves for garnishing

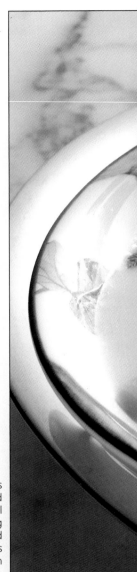

Chervil, with its delicate, slightly aniseed flavor, goes very well with this egg yolk–thickened asparagus soup and its exquisite crayfish garnish.

1. Bring a large pot of lightly salted water to a roiling boil. Add the crayfish to the pot one after the other and boil for 5–6 minutes,

making sure that the water is always at a roiling boil before the next one is added. Remove the crayfish and let cool. To extract the meat from the shells, twist the tail off the body, taking care to leave the tail meat as intact as possible. Grasp the tail fan between your thumb and index finger, twist away from the body, and carefully pull out the attached intestine. Bend open the shell

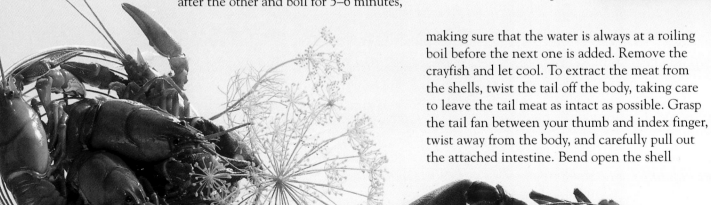

lengthwise so that the thin underside tears, or cut open the shell on its underside. Remove the meat. Twist off the claws, then carefully crack them open and remove the meat; set aside.

2. Cut off the bottom ends of the asparagus. Using a knife or a vegetable peeler, pare the stalks from top to bottom, starting right under the tip and peeling more thickly toward the end of the stalk. Wash the peelings and trimmed-off ends, place in a pot with about 4½ cups of water (enough to cover), salt lightly, and bring to a boil. Reduce heat and simmer for about 20 minutes. Remove from heat, take out the stalks and set aside, and strain through a fine-mesh sieve.

3. Boil the asparagus stalks in the reserved stock until *al dente*, then remove. Cut the stalks into 1½-inch-long sections, starting at the tips, and set aside.

4. Return the stock to a boil with ⅓ cup of cream. Lower the heat, and reduce to about 3 cups. Add the crayfish meat and the asparagus pieces. Whisk the remaining cream with the egg yolks and stir into the soup; do not let it boil, or the yolk will curdle. Season to taste with salt, pepper, and nutmeg. Ladle into 4 bowls, spoon one-fourth of the rice into each, and serve garnished with chervil.

Beer soups
An almost forgotten aspect of the "German national drink" — as a basis for hot soups

If one looks for such recipes, you will find them mainly in the cookbooks of yore. There is a reason for this: in the (often not so) good old days, a beer soup enriched with bread, sago, eggs, or other garnishes (especially during the winter) was a fortifying source of energy — simple and quick to prepare and also cheap to make. Most of the ingredients were at hand, and many people brewed beer in their own cellars. This was also the case for many monasteries, where beer soups were served as a food during fasts. And the more different the region and people, the more varied their preferences for certain specialties from the beer cellar, both then and now. For example, over 200 years ago people in Friesland often made a soup of brown ale, which they occasionally even consumed at breakfast. Even if this is not much to our taste nowadays, it is still worthwhile to sample this soup, perhaps at a more suitable time of day. In Bavaria, by contrast, people have always been fond of the pale, top-fermented *weiss* (white) beer — also known as wheat beer (because it is brewed from the latter grain rather than barley) — for their soups as well as for drinking. Only lightly hopped, it tastes comparatively unbitter and is even compatible with a spice mixture of cloves, cinnamon, and ginger, as the recipe on this page demonstrates.

Genuine sago is obtained from the starchy pith of a tropical variety of palm. Traditionally, it has been used as a soup garnish, or as a thickening agent in sweet dishes and desserts.

FRISIAN BEER SOUP
(not pictured)
Serves 4
5 oz sliced dark rye bread, cut into ½-inch cubes
4 cups brown ale
2 eggs, pinch sugar, salt

1. Place the bread cubes in a bowl, pour in the beer, and let soak for 30 minutes.

2. Push the softened bread cubes with the beer through a fine-mesh sieve into a pot and bring to a boil. Remove from heat.

3. Beat the eggs together with the sugar in a bowl, then fold into the beer soup. Season with salt, adding additional sugar if necessary. Return to heat but do not bring to a boil again, as this would cause the egg yolk to curdle. Serve immediately.

WHITE BEER SOUP
Serves 4
4½ cups pale (white) beer
10 teaspoons sugar, 2 teaspoons lemon juice
grated rind of ½ lemon
1 clove, 1 small piece cinnamon stick
pinch ground ginger, 2½ oz sago
For the garnish:
Lemon balm leaves

1. Bring the beer to a boil with the sugar, lemon juice, lemon rind, clove, cinnamon stick, and ginger.

2. Wash and drain the sago. As soon as the beer comes to a boil, sprinkle in the sago, reduce heat, and simmer for 40 minutes (long enough to cook the sago). Garnish with lemon balm leaves before serving.

To serve the white beer soup, ladle it into soup bowls and sprinkle with lemon balm leaves, which, together with the lemon rind and juice, add a tart undercurrent to this dish.

Westphalian bigosch

A warming winter stew with fresh and pickled cabbage, pork, and Mettwurst (smoked sausage)

In the 19th century, when people from present-day Poland, mainly Pomerania and Silesia, arrived in the coal-mining region of Westphalia in search of work, they brought with them the recipe for their national dish, *bigos*, a stew containing pork, white cabbage, sauerkraut, sausage, and fresh wild mushrooms — ingredients that are also indispensable to the down-to-earth, hearty cooking of Westphalia. It is not surprising then that this dish was naturalized in the Ruhr area as Westphalian *bigosch*. Kielbasa — the heartily seasoned pork sausage with paprika and garlic that was used in the original Polish recipe — was no longer available, but this was not a problem in the land of ham and sausage; cooks simply fell back on a Westphalian specialty, *mettendchen*, small pork sausages seasoned with salt and pepper and sold dried or smoked. The smoked variety harmonizes particularly well with this recipe, since it intensifies the flavor of the smoked bacon. Boiled potatoes or hearty farmhouse bread are the recommended accompaniment for *bigosch*. Typical Westphalian beverages are served (though not exclusively) with the dish: a dry Pilsner with the meal, a well-chilled schnapps as an aperitif, and a pure-grain brandy or a *steinhäger* (gin-style schnapps).

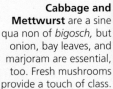

Cabbage and Mettwurst are a sine qua non of *bigosch,* but onion, bay leaves, and marjoram are essential, too. Fresh mushrooms provide a touch of class.

Serves 4

7½ teaspoons butter, 1 tablespoon oil
7 oz pork shoulder, cut into ¾-inch cubes
7 oz uncooked smoked bacon, cut into ¾-inch cubes
4 Mettwurst sausages, sliced ½-inch thick
1½ cups finely chopped onion
7 oz white cabbage, grated or sliced into thin strips
¾ cup sauerkraut, slightly separated
2 crushed garlic cloves
1 teaspoon chopped marjoram, 1 teaspoon caraway seeds
½ teaspoon Hungarian paprika
salt, freshly ground pepper
1 bay leaf, 1 tablespoon tomato paste

8½ oz fresh mushrooms, whole or halved (depending on size)

1. Preheat the oven to 350⁰. Heat the butter and oil in a large, flameproof pot; add the pork and sauté on all sides until lightly browned. Add the bacon, sausages, and onion, and continue to sauté for 1–2 minutes.

2. Layer the cabbage and sauerkraut on top of the meat and add the garlic. Season with marjoram, caraway seeds, paprika, salt, and pepper, and add the bay leaf.

3. Stir the tomato paste together with about 1½ cups of water and pour this over the contents of the pot, which should now be barely covered with liquid. Cover, and bake the stew for about 90 minutes, adding a little extra water if necessary.

4. Remove the pot from the oven 15 minutes before the end of cooking time, stir in the mushrooms, and bake until done. Serve while steaming hot.

Millet is one of the oldest cultivated grains, and a staple food in many of the world's countries. Although wheat and rice have, to a large extent, usurped its place in Europe, it is currently undergoing a revival as a whole food due to its rich mineral content. Millet is available as "gold millet" (whole grains), or as cracked millet, flakes, or flour.

Vegetable bouillon with millet dumplings

A clear soup garnished with fluffy dumplings — an appetizing start to a meal

The success of the millet dumplings, and indeed of all similar soup garnishes, depends to a large extent on the accurate preparation and careful shaping and cooking of the dumpling mixture. It is advisable to prepare 1 or 2 test dumplings and then simmer them gently for several minutes to make sure that they keep their shape. If they fail to hold together, add a little more flour and an egg to the mixture.

Serves 4
For the millet dumplings:
¾ cup millet flour
generous pinch curry powder
salt, freshly ground pepper
10 teaspoons softened butter, in small curls
10 teaspoons vegetable stock
2 eggs, 2 tablespoons flour
For the bouillon:
3½ cups vegetable stock
salt, freshly ground white pepper
½ cup scallions, sliced into thin rounds
1 cup carrots, diced into ¼-inch pieces

You will also need:
8½ oz tomatoes, blanched, skinned, seeded, and cut into ¼-inch pieces
handful watercress, torn into bite-sized pieces

1. To make the dumplings, briefly dry-roast the millet flour in a heavy pan with the curry powder, salt, and pepper. Add the butter, stirring it into the flour. Gradually add about 3 tablespoons of the vegetable stock, stirring until the flour forms a ball. Remove from heat and let the dough cool. Mix the eggs into the dough one at a time. Knead in the flour and the remaining vegetable stock and set aside.

2. For the bouillon, heat the vegetable stock in a large pot with 1 cup of water and season with salt and pepper. Add the scallions and carrots, and bring to a low boil.

3. Using two wet teaspoons, shape the millet mixture into approximately 30 small dumplings. Gently lower these into the bouillon, reduce heat, and simmer for 10–15 minutes.

4. Add the tomatoes and watercress to the bouillon for the final 2 minutes of cooking time. Adjust the seasonings, ladle into bowls, and serve.

Bremen chicken ragout

Fleurons, delicate but simple puff pastry garnishes, are the traditional accompaniment for this dish

Serves 6

7 oz veal sweetbreads, 2 chickens (about 1⅓ lb each)
1 bunch chopped vegetables (2 carrots, 1 leek, 2 onions, 2 celery sticks, 2 parsley stalks)
salt, 5 white peppercorns
3 tablespoons sherry vinegar
8 crayfish (about 3 oz each), dash lemon juice
1¼ lb chopped white asparagus (reserve the tips)
1¼ lb (preshelled weight) fresh, shelled peas
freshly ground white pepper
½ cup butter, 1½ oz small, fresh morel mushrooms
2 tablespoons flour, ½ cup cream and 2 egg yolks whisked together
For the garnish:
1 tablespoon chopped parsley

1. Soak the sweetbreads for 2 hours. Wash the chickens; remove, skin, halve, and refrigerate the breasts. Boil the remaining chicken, vegetables, and spices in 6½ cups of water. Simmer,

An honor roll of select ingredients for a truly exquisite stew. The chicken breasts, sweetbreads, and morel mushrooms — together with the braising liquid — are reheated in the sauce with all the other garnishes before the ragout is sprinkled with parsley and served.

uncovered, while skimming for 30 minutes. Skin and strip the meat from the legs and dice. Cook the sweetbreads and vinegar in boiling water for 10 minutes; then rinse and chop up, removing all membranes and veins.

2. Boil the crayfish for 4 minutes. Cool, extract all the meat, and set aside.

3. Remove the remaining chicken from the stock and discard. Strain the stock and set aside 4 cups. Simmer the remainder with the lemon juice, asparagus (not the tips), and peas for 5 minutes. Add the tips; simmer for 5 minutes. Remove the asparagus and peas. Season the

chicken breasts with salt and pepper and sauté in 10 teaspoons of butter. Add the sweetbreads and mushrooms (both salted) and braise, covered, for 5 minutes.

4. Simmer the remaining butter and flour without letting it brown. Stir in the reserved stock; bring to a boil. Reduce heat and simmer for 10 minutes. Add the asparagus, peas, and cream and egg yolk mixture; do not let it boil. Adjust the seasonings, ladle into bowls, and garnish with parsley before serving.

Cream of watercress soup

The tangy, piquant, radishlike flavor of the watercress is complemented perfectly by a hefty dollop of cream

Rapeseed or canola oil, suggested here for sautéing the vegetables, still has the image of an oil that one falls back on in hard times. Until about 20 years ago this was justified, since up until then rapeseed oil contained a high amount of erucic acid, which is not well suited for human consumption. In the 1970s, however, new varieties of rapeseed were bred that contained only trace quantities of erucic acid, and nowadays rapeseed can be used as an all-purpose oil. Like other edible oils, it is available both unrefined and refined. "Virgin" or unrefined rapeseed oil can be recognized by the words "cold pressed" or "first pressing" on the label; a special pressing process preserves the distinctive odor, flavor, and color. If the flavor of the virgin oil is too strong, choose the refined instead.

Serves 4
3 tablespoons canola or rapeseed oil
¾ cup diced onion
10½ oz potatoes, diced into ¼-inch pieces
3½ cups chicken stock
10½ oz coarsely chopped watercress leaves
salt, freshly ground pepper
freshly grated nutmeg
10 teaspoons cream and 2 egg yolks, whisked together
For the garnish:
½ cup heavy cream
a few watercress leaves

1. Heat the canola oil in a pot and sauté the onion without letting it brown. Add the potatoes and sauté briefly, stirring from time to time. Pour in the chicken stock and bring to a boil. Reduce heat and simmer for 15 minutes.

2. Stir in the watercress and simmer for another 15 minutes. Season with salt, pepper, and nutmeg. Remove from heat.

3. Finely purée the soup with a handheld blender. Stir in the cream and egg yolk mixture. Reheat without letting it boil, as this would cause the egg yolk to curdle. Adjust the seasonings.

4. Whip the cream until it forms soft peaks. Ladle the soup into heated soup plates and garnish with a dollop of cream and a few watercress leaves before serving.

Watercress, canola oil, and potatoes are the main ingredients for an exquisite cream of watercress soup that not only tastes delicious, but is good for you, too.

With its distinctive, large cap, the portobello mushroom, here a variety from Holland, is a relative of the universally popular cultivated mushroom. Before adding in the mushrooms, the gills should be removed as they would otherwise make the soup too dark.

Portobello mushroom soup

A fine cream of mushroom soup, garnished with deep-fried, mini bread dumplings

Portobello mushrooms, with their rich, earthy flavor and hearty texture are featured in this soup. If their flavor is too strong, however, other mushrooms may be used.

Serves 4
For the deep-fried bread dumplings:
4 slices day-old white bread, cut into small cubes
¼ cup lukewarm milk, ⅙ cup finely chopped onion,
1 egg yolk
1 tablespoon chopped herbs (parsley, chives)
salt, freshly ground white pepper
vegetable oil for deep-frying
For the soup:
1¼ lb portobello mushrooms, ¼ cup butter
1¼ cup finely chopped onion, 2 cups veal stock,
1⅛ cups cream
salt, freshly ground white pepper
dash lemon juice, 1 tablespoon chopped parsley
For the garnish:
7 oz portobello mushrooms, 5 teaspoons butter
2 tablespoons unsweetened whipped cream

1. First, prepare dumplings: Place the bread cubes in a bowl and pour in the milk. Mix the onion, egg yolk, and herbs in with the bread; season with salt and pepper; and blend together well. Shape the mixture into 20 small dumplings, place in a bowl, cover, and refrigerate.

2. To make the soup, using a paring knife, pull the skin off the mushrooms and cut out their stems; scrape out the gills with a melon baller or a pointy teaspoon. Cut the caps and stalks up small. Heat the butter in a pot and sauté the onion without letting it brown. Add the mushrooms and continue to sauté for 2–3 minutes. Pour in the veal stock and bring to a boil. Reduce heat and simmer for 15 minutes. Add the cream and simmer for another 5 minutes. Season with salt, pepper, and lemon juice. Blend the soup with a handheld blender until very smooth. Sprinkle in the parsley and keep warm.

3. For the garnish, trim the mushrooms as described above and slice the caps. Heat the butter and briefly fry the mushroom slices on both sides.

4. Heat the oil to 325⁰ and deep-fry the dumplings for 3–4 minutes, until golden brown. Remove and drain on paper towels. Fold in the whipped cream, garnish with the sautéed mushrooms, add the dumplings, and serve.

In the Alpine regions
it is usually the gray-brown *Braunvieh* cattle that supply the milk from which spicy cheeses such as Mondseer are made.

Cheese soup
Warming and substantial, this soup can be a meal in itself

The Salzkammergut, a district of outstanding natural beauty in northern Austria to the east of Salzburg, is home to the cheese that is particularly suitable for this hearty winter soup: Mondseer, also know as *Schachtelk* (box cheese). Mondseer is a semisoft cheese with sparse, red surface bacteria and a light-yellow, soft interior. It tastes strong and spicy, occasionally a bit tangy. As it is not always available, Tilsit, Trappist cheese, or *Almk*, as well as Danish Esrom, may be substituted if need be, though this will of course alter the flavor of the soup accordingly.

Serves 4
¼ cup butter
½ cup diced onion, 1 diced garlic clove
2 tablespoons flour
4½ cups hot beef stock
5½ oz semisoft cheese (preferably Mondseer), rind removed and coarsely shredded
1 teaspoon caraway seeds
salt, freshly ground white pepper
For the croutons:
7½ teaspoons butter
4 slices day-old white bread, cut into cubes
You will also need:
3½ oz semisoft cheese (preferably Mondseer), cut into strips
1 bunch finely chopped chives

1. Melt the butter in a pot and sauté the onion and garlic until translucent. Sprinkle in the flour and continue sautéing, stirring frequently, until lightly browned. Pour in the beef stock and bring to a boil. Reduce heat and simmer for about 15 minutes.

2. Stir the cheese into the soup and return briefly to a boil, then reduce heat. Add the caraway seeds and season with salt and pepper. Keep the soup hot.

3. For the croutons, melt the butter in a small frying pan and brown the bread cubes on all sides.

4. Preheat the oven to broil. Ladle the soup into ovenproof soup plates and top with the croutons and cheese strips. Heat the soup in the oven until the cheese melts. Sprinkle the chives on top and serve immediately while the croutons are still nice and crunchy.

Garlic, caraway seeds, and chives — aside from the cheese, of course — give this soup its hearty flavor. For a nice accompaniment, choose a well-chilled white wine; a strong and fruity one would be ideal.

Tafelspitz bouillon with liver dumplings

The bouillon, in which the beef gently simmers, is a delight in itself, while the meat makes an exquisite garnish for the soup

Serves 6–8
For the bouillon:
1 small onion; 1 teaspoon salt; 3 lb bottom round beef
1 bay leaf, 5 white peppercorns
5 parsley stalks
1 cup carrots, ⅔ cup each celeriac and leeks, all chopped
For the liver dumplings:
4 day-old white rolls, salt
1⅛ cups lukewarm milk, 7 oz ox liver
½ cup finely diced onion, 7½ teaspoons butter, 1 tablespoon chopped parsley
2 eggs, freshly ground pepper, 1 teaspoon chopped marjoram, grated rind from 1 lemon
For the vegetable garnish:
¾ cup cauliflower florets
¼ cup celeriac, ½ cup carrots and leeks, all thinly sliced; 5½ oz (unshelled weight) freshly shelled peas
⅓ cup zucchini, thinly sliced into 2-inch strips
For the garnish:
2 tablespoons finely diced chives

1. Caramelize the onion (cut in two and place both halves cut-surface down on a heated pan until they turn dark brown). In a large pot, boil 11 cups of water with the salt, beef, bay leaf, peppercorns, parsley stalks, and the onion halves. Reduce heat and simmer for 1½–2 hours, skimming off frequently. Add the carrots, celeriac, and leeks about 40 minutes before the end of cooking time.

2. To make the dumplings, slice the rolls, season with salt, pour over the milk, and let soak, covered, in the refrigerator. Rinse the ox liver and peel off the membrane; purée with the onion. Heat the butter and sauté the parsley. Squeeze out the rolls and make dough with the parsley, purée, and remaining dumpling ingredients. Shape into small dumplings and boil gently for 10 minutes, then simmer for another 5–10 minutes.

3. Boil the cauliflower for 5 minutes. Add first the celeriac and carrots, then the leeks and peas, and the zucchini last, at 1-minute intervals, blanching the zucchini for an additional minute. Remove the vegetables and rinse in cold water.

4. Remove the beef from the bouillon and slice. Strain the bouillon, adjust the seasonings, and reheat. Add the beef and vegetables and warm through. Ladle into bowls, add the dumplings, and garnish with chives before serving.

Yellow split peas, used instead of whole peas normally found in this recipe, reduce the usual cooking time of this soup by about half.

Swiss market soup

A dish of split peas, pickled pork, and vegetables that really sticks to the ribs

This specialty comes from Bern, the Swiss capital, and is often referred to as "Bernese pea soup." It is called "market" soup because originally it was made primarily on market days — and after a leisurely stroll around the market, especially on a cold, rainy day, it was just perfect to come home to. The most typical ingredients are the dried, split yellow peas, which provide its appetizing color, and a pickled pork knuckle, known affectionately (as well as graphically) in Swiss-German as *gnagi*.

The pork knuckle and bacon add a great deal of heartiness and flavor to the soup, so season with restraint.

Serves 4
½ cup dried, split yellow peas
6½ cup unsalted beef bouillon
1 pickled pork knuckle (about 1¾ lb)
5 teaspoons butter
⅔ cup finely diced, uncooked bacon
⅔ cup finely chopped onion
¾ cup leeks, cut into thin rings
⅔ cup celeriac, diced into ½-inch pieces
1 cup thinly sliced carrots
8½ oz potatoes, cut into ½-inch cubes
1 bay leaf
2 thyme sprigs

salt, freshly ground pepper
For the garnish:
2 tablespoons finely diced chives

1. Rinse the peas under cold water. Transfer to a bowl with enough cold water to cover, and let soak overnight. The next day, pour off the water and drain well. Set the drained peas aside.

2. Bring the beef bouillon to a boil in a large pot. Lower in the pork knuckle, reduce heat, and simmer for 1½ hours.

3. Add the reserved peas to the pot and simmer for another 15 minutes. Keep warm.

4. Melt the butter in a frying pan and cook the bacon until the fat can be swirled around. Add the onion and sauté until translucent, stirring occasionally. Add the leeks, celeriac, and carrots, and sauté briefly.

5. Transfer the bacon-vegetable mixture to the pot with the pork knuckle and stir well. Add the potatoes, bay leaf, and thyme sprigs and simmer for another 25–30 minutes. If necessary, add a bit more beef bouillon. Season with salt and pepper.

6. Remove the pork knuckle from the pot, separate the meat from the bone, and cut into pieces. Pour the soup into a tureen and add the meat back to the soup. Before serving, garnish with the chives.

Cream soup with leeks

Having a flavorful, homemade chicken broth as the base

To include pieces of chicken in this soup, after preparing the broth, remove the skin, separate the meat from the bones, cut into bite-sized pieces, and add to the soup before serving; otherwise use the meat in another recipe.

Serves 4
For about 3½ qt chicken broth:
1 prepared boiling chicken (4½–5½ lb)
2¼ lb sliced veal bones, 20 peppercorns
2 crushed garlic cloves
1 small onion studded with 4 cloves
For the bouquet garni:
¾ cup carrots, ⅔ cup leeks, ⅓ cup celery, all chopped
2 bay leaves, 2 thyme sprigs, 6 parsley stalks
For the soup:
10 teaspoons butter
2 cups leeks (white part only), cut up small; ½ cup diced celery
2 tablespoons flour, ¾ cup cream
salt, freshly ground pepper, freshly grated nutmeg
5 teaspoons cold butter, in small pieces
For the garnish:
5 teaspoons butter, ⅔ cup leeks, sliced into thin rings, salt, freshly ground pepper

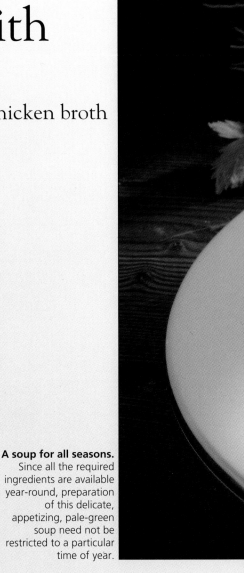

A soup for all seasons. Since all the required ingredients are available year-round, preparation of this delicate, appetizing, pale-green soup need not be restricted to a particular time of year.

1. Wash the chicken thoroughly then drain and cut into four pieces. Place in a pot with the veal bones and cover with water. Boil until the protein and impurities rise to the surface. Pour off the liquid and rinse the chicken pieces and veal bones with warm water. Add back to the pot with 4½ qt of fresh water and bring to a boil, skimming repeatedly. Reduce heat to just under boiling and simmer for 3 hours. After 2 hours stir in the peppercorns, garlic, studded onion, and the bouquet garni; add water if necessary.

2. Remove the chicken pieces from the broth. Remove the broth from heat, line a conical sieve with cheesecloth, and pour the broth through. Let cool and skim off the fat. Measure off 4½ cups for the soup; the remainder can be frozen.

3. For the soup, melt the butter in a pot and sauté the leeks and celery until translucent. Sprinkle in the flour and sauté for 1–2 minutes without letting it brown. Pour in the reserved broth, stir until smooth, and bring to a boil. Reduce heat and simmer for 20 minutes. Stir in the cream and season with salt, pepper, and

nutmeg. Remove from heat, purée until smooth, and return to the pot. Reheat and stir in the butter. Keep warm.

4. To make the garnish, heat the butter and sauté the leeks for 3–4 minutes. Season with salt and pepper.

5. Ladle the soup into warmed bowls and garnish with the leeks, adding the pieces of cooked chicken if desired. Serve piping hot.

Mushroom stew with venison dumplings

An autumn meal par excellence, whose bold flavors are nicely accompanied by a red Valtellina

Serves 4

For about 6½ cups game stock:
2¼ lb game bones, 1 tablespoon vegetable oil
1 bay leaf, 1 clove, 6 white peppercorns
3 juniper berries, 1 thyme sprig
For the bouquet garni:
½ cup chopped carrots, ½ cup chopped parsley root
⅓ cup chopped leeks, 1 chopped garlic clove
For the game dumplings:
5½ oz venison (from the haunch), cut into pieces
5½ oz pork shoulder, cut into pieces
¼ cup diced onion, 1 diced garlic clove
4 allspice berries, 1 juniper berry
5 black peppercorns, ½ bay leaf
1 tablespoon chopped herbs (thyme, parsley)
1 egg, 1 tablespoon white bread crumbs, ⅛ cup cream
For the stew:
7½ teaspoons butter, ⅓ cup finely chopped scallions
1 cup diced carrots
¾ cup diced celeriac, ½ cup diced parsley root
1¼ lb potatoes, cut into ½-inch chunks
salt, freshly ground pepper
1 bay leaf, 5 juniper berries
1½ lb chopped fresh mushrooms
2 tablespoons chopped, flat-leaf (Italian) parsley
For the garnish:
½ cup heavy cream blended with ½ teaspoon buttermilk (crème fraîche)

1. To make the game stock, preheat the oven to 350⁰. Wash and chop up the game bones and place in a roasting pan with the vegetable oil. Brown the bones on all sides, then remove and drain. Transfer the bones to a large stockpot and add enough cold water to cover. Bring to a boil, skimming frequently. Add the herbs and spices, and the bouquet garni. Reduce heat and simmer for 1½ hours. Remove from heat, line a conical sieve with cheesecloth, and strain the stock. Let cool and skim off the fat. Reserve 5¼ cups for the stew.

2. To make the dumplings, blend or process the venison, pork, onion, and garlic. Grind the allspice and juniper berries, peppercorns, and bay leaf to a very fine powder with a mortar and pestle. Mix the dumpling ingredients together and knead to a smooth dough. Shape into 16 small dumplings.

3. For the stew, melt the butter and sauté the scallions until translucent. Add the carrots, celeriac, parsley root, and potatoes and briefly simmer. Pour in the prepared game stock and season with salt and pepper. Add the bay leaf and juniper berries and bring to a boil. Reduce heat and simmer for 15 minutes. Add the mushrooms and simmer for another 4–5 minutes. Sprinkle in the parsley and adjust the seasonings. Keep warm.

4. Boil the dumplings in salted water, reduce heat, and simmer for 10 minutes, until done. Carefully remove, drain, and gently add to the stew. Ladle into 4 soup plates, and garnish each with a dollop of crème fraîche before serving.

Fresh sheep's milk is essential for the production of pecorino. Made chiefly in central and southern Italy, this spicy, hard cheese can add the crowning touch to a dish, freshly grated over pasta or a hearty soup.

Minestrone from Campania

The classic Italian soup par excellence — here in a version from the southwest of the country

Minestrone is surely one of the world's most famous vegetable soups — a claim that can be made without fear of exaggeration. And, as is always the case with classics, widely varying versions of this soup are made from region to region. This is hardly surprising for a soup prepared according to the basic principle of "straight from the vegetable garden," making use of whatever is in season. In Campania, fresh vegetables are available nearly all year, with an amazing variety and quantity flourishing in the fertile fields around Vesuvius. Unlike the minestrone of the north, which is often made with dried white beans, this version from the *mezzogiorno*, the south of Italy, is made exclusively with fresh vegetables.

Serves 4
½ cup finely diced, uncooked bacon
2 thinly sliced garlic cloves
¾ cup onion, sliced into rings
9 cups vegetable stock
7 oz green beans, halved or cut into thirds (depending on size)
1⅓ cups carrots, diced into ½-inch pieces
1¼ cups celeriac, diced into ½-inch pieces
14 oz potatoes, cut into ½-inch cubes
⅔ cup leeks, sliced into ½-inch rings
10½ oz Savoy cabbage, sliced into ½-inch-thick strips
8½ oz (unshelled weight) fresh, shelled peas (about 4 oz shelled weight)
3½ oz soup pasta (e.g. ditali piccoli rigati)
2 tablespoons chopped parsley
1 tablespoon fresh basil, cut into strips
salt, freshly ground pepper
For the garnish:
basil leaves
2 tablespoons freshly grated, aged pecorino (optional)

1. Fry the bacon in a pot until the fat can be swirled around. Add the garlic and onion and sauté without letting them brown. Pour in the vegetable stock and bring to a boil. Reduce heat and simmer for 20 minutes.

2. Add the beans, carrots, celeriac, and potatoes to the soup and simmer for 10 minutes. Add the leeks and cabbage and simmer for another 5 minutes. Finally, stir in the peas and pasta and simmer for 10 minutes more.

3. Sprinkle in the parsley and basil, and season with salt and pepper. Ladle into soup plates, garnish with basil leaves, and serve immediately, sprinkled with grated pecorino if desired.

Cream of zucchini soup

Served with stuffed zucchini flowers — a delight for both the eyes and the palate

Serves 4
3 zucchini (about 1 lb)
10 teaspoons butter
1 diced garlic clove, ⅔ cup diced white onion
2⅔ cups veal stock
1 thyme sprig, salt, freshly ground pepper
½ cup cream
For the stuffed zucchini flowers:
8 zucchini flowers, 3 tablespoons olive oil,
3 oz finely diced ham
⅓ cup white onion, 1 garlic clove, both finely diced
⅜ cup finely diced eggplant
1⅓ cups diced bell peppers (red, yellow, or green)
3½ oz plum tomatoes, blanched, skinned, seeded,
and finely diced
salt, freshly ground pepper
1 tablespoon chopped herbs (sage, parsley, thyme,
rosemary)

Thyme is one of the most quintessentially Mediterranean herbs. It is native to the scrublands of those countries, where the wild variety grows luxuriantly.

The hearty stuffing of the zucchini flowers creates a most interesting flavor counterpoint to this mild cream soup.

For the garnish:
thyme leaves

1. Wash the zucchini and cut off the stalk and flower ends. Using a small melon baller, scoop "pearls" from one of the zucchini and set aside. Cut the remaining zucchini into ½-inch pieces.

2. Melt the butter in a pot and sauté the zucchini pieces, garlic, and onion for 3–4 minutes. Pour in the veal stock, add the thyme, and season with salt and pepper. Simmer, covered, for 15 minutes.

3. Remove from heat and take out the thyme sprig. Purée the contents of the pot in a blender,

then pour back into the pot. Return to heat and stir in the cream. Simmer for 10 minutes, then adjust the seasonings.

4. Simmer the zucchini "pearls" in lightly salted water for 3–4 minutes; remove, drain well, and add to the soup. Keep warm.

5. For the stuffed zucchini flowers, carefully open the calyx and remove the pistil using a small, sharp knife. Set aside.

6. Heat the olive oil in a pan and sauté the ham, onion, and garlic until lightly browned. Add the eggplant and peppers and sauté for another 1–2

minutes. Stir in the tomatoes, reduce heat, and braise for 10 minutes. Season with salt and pepper and sprinkle in the herbs. Let cool slightly.

7. Using a teaspoon, stuff the flowers with the ham and vegetable mixture. Twist the tips of the flowers together to seal. Wrap the flowers in plastic wrap, tie with string, and simmer gently in lightly boiling water for 5 minutes.

8. Ladle the soup into plates. Remove the zucchini flowers from the water, take off the plastic wrap, and arrange two flowers in each bowl. Garnish with thyme leaves and serve immediately.

Spinach soup with rice

A beef broth is the basis of this light *Minestra Marià*, as enjoyed in Piedmont and the Valle d'Aosta

To prepare this soup — whose lightness and digestibility almost place it in the category of "convalescent food," you don't really need many different ingredients, or particularly unusual ones. But, precisely because of this, the quality of each individual ingredient is crucial: the spinach must be really young and tender, the broth both substantial and flavorful, and the cheese strong and spicy.

Serves 4
1½ lb young leaf spinach, salt
10 teaspoons butter
⅓ cup finely chopped onion, 1 finely chopped garlic clove
⅝ cup long-grain rice
4½ cups beef broth
freshly ground pepper, 1 egg
4½ teaspoons freshly grated Parmesan
You will also need:
freshly grated Parmesan

1. Wash the spinach thoroughly and remove the thick stalks. Blanch the leaves in boiling, salted water until just wilted, then remove, drain, and lightly squeeze out the water. Let cool, coarsely chop, and set aside.

2. Heat the butter in a pot and sauté the onion and garlic without letting them brown. Add the rice and sauté until transparent. Pour in the beef broth and bring to a boil. Reduce heat and simmer for 15–20 minutes, adding the reserved spinach during the last 5 minutes of cooking time. Season the soup with salt and pepper.

3. Whisk the egg in a soup tureen and mix in the Parmesan. Ladle in one-third of the hot soup and stir to blend. Mix in the remaining soup and serve immediately. Pass additional Parmesan around for sprinkling on top.

Freshly grated Parmesan is an essential seasoning for this simple soup, so make sure there is enough to pass around the table. The egg, which is whisked in a tureen with some of the cheese before the soup is stirred in, makes the dish a touch more nourishing and substantial.

Mussel soup

Mussels and plenty of vegetables, gently simmered in mussel juices, fish stock, and white wine

It's not surprising that black-shelled mussels with their bright-orange flesh are so popular in Venice and surrounding areas, since they are available there from April to September fresh from the lagoon, where large-scale mussel farming takes place. Visible everywhere are the posts that rise out of the water, on which lines for the nets are hung. It is in these nets that the mollusks grow for about 1½ years before they are harvested.

Serves 4
3½ lb mussels
3 tablespoons olive oil
1 cup thinly sliced white onion
3 finely chopped garlic cloves
1 cup white wine, 3½ cups fish stock
1¼ lb tomatoes, blanched, skinned, seeded, and diced (reserve the seeds)
1 cup thinly sliced carrots
coarse sea salt, coarsely ground black pepper
3 tablespoons chopped parsley

To serve, ladle the soup into heated bowls, add the remaining (unshucked) mussels, sprinkle with chopped parsley, and pass around the garlic bread as an accompaniment.

For the toasted garlic bread:
5 tablespoons extra virgin olive oil
3 garlic cloves
4–8 slices Italian bread

1. Thoroughly scrub the mussels under cold water to remove any sand or residue. Pull off and discard the beards. Throw away any open mussels, as these could be spoiled.

2. Heat the olive oil in a large pot and sauté the onion and garlic until lightly browned. Add the mussels and pour in the wine. Cover, and simmer

until all the mussels are open — about 7–8 minutes — shaking the pot vigorously several times. Discard any mussels that remain closed, as they could be spoiled. Remove the mussels and onion with a slotted spoon and set aside. Pour the mussel liquid through a very fine sieve or cheesecloth to filter any remaining sand.

3. Combine the mussel liquid and fish stock in a large pot and slowly bring to a boil. In the meantime, strain the tomato seeds through a sieve, collecting the juice, and add this to the stock. Stir the tomatoes and carrots into the stock, and simmer for about 10 minutes.

4. Shuck two-thirds of the mussels, and add the meat and reserved onion to the soup. Season with salt and pepper.

5. For the garlic bread, preheat the oven to 390–400°. Pour the olive oil into a small bowl. Squeeze the garlic through a press into the oil and stir well to mix. Brush one side of the bread slices with the garlic oil, place on a baking sheet, and toast until golden brown.

Cream of arugula soup

With a crispy garnish that's a bit out of the ordinary —
arugula leaves, deep-fried in olive oil

Arugula — also known as rugola or rocket — grows wild in Central European latitudes, and was valued in Germany as far back as the Middle Ages both as a condiment and for medicinal purposes. But it was only via a circuitous route — through Italian cooking that is so very popular — that it was once more restored to culinary glory. The notched leaves with their pleasantly hot, slightly bitter taste are predominantly consumed raw — in salads or as a pesto ingredient. What is less well known, however, is that they also taste good cooked. For this soup, they are actually deep-fried, which gives them an especially delicate, nutty flavor.

Serves 4
1½ cups extra virgin olive oil
7 oz finely chopped arugula leaves
7½ teaspoons butter
⅝ cup finely chopped shallots
1 finely chopped garlic clove
4½ teaspoons flour
½ cup white wine
2¼ cups chicken stock
1⅛ cups cream
salt
cayenne pepper

1. Heat the olive oil in a pot and deep-fry the arugula in batches until crisp. Remove, and drain well on paper towels. Reserve a few leaves for the garnish, and cut the remaining leaves into small pieces. Set aside.

2. Heat the butter in a pot and sauté the shallots and garlic until translucent. Sprinkle in the flour and continue sautéing, stirring frequently, without letting it brown. Add the wine, simmer, and stir until smooth.

3. Add the chicken stock, mixing continuously; stir the mixture until smooth and simmer for 10 minutes. Pour in the cream and simmer briefly. Season with salt and cayenne pepper and stir in the reserved, chopped arugula.

4. Remove from heat, finely purée in a blender, and strain the soup through a sieve back into the pot. Bring to a boil, adjust the seasonings, and blend with an eggbeater or handheld blender until foamy. Ladle the soup into heated soup plates and serve garnished with the deep-fried arugula leaves.

Deep-fried arugula leaves — when preparing this unusual soup garnish, take care to dry the leaves thoroughly between paper towels or in a salad spinner before deep-frying them — otherwise you may get splattered with hot oil!

Fennel soup

Zuppa di finocchio: Light and refreshing, and topped with toasted slices of bread

Whitish, aromatic fennel bulbs are available in Europe chiefly from October to May. Depending on the variety, they can either be plump or elongate in shape; either way, the flavor is the same. When buying, make sure that the cut stalk ends are not dried, and that the feathery, green leaves look fresh and shiny — it would be a pity to have to throw these away. Finely chopped, not only can they be used as additional seasoning for a fennel soup, but their sweetish, slightly hot flavor also lends a novel touch (to a cucumber salad, for example).

Serves 4
2 tablespoons olive oil
⅜ cup diced, uncooked bacon
½ cup diced white onion, 1¼ lb diced fennel bulbs
2 tablespoons tomato paste
4½ cups veal stock, salt

Characteristic fennel flavor (with its powerful aniseed taste) is introduced in this soup not only by the bulbs, but also the chopped fresh leaves of this herb.

1 tablespoon each chopped parsley and fennel leaves
For the toasted bread:
4–8 slices (depending on size) Italian bread
5 tablespoons extra virgin olive oil

Many housewives in the southern regions of Italy still prepare their own tomato paste. This is done by spreading puréed tomato pulp on a board and placing it in the blazing sun until the desired concentration is achieved.

You will also need:
2 tablespoons freshly grated pecorino
1 tablespoon chopped parsley and fennel leaves

1. Heat the olive oil in a pot and fry the bacon. Add the onion and fennel and sauté until translucent. Quickly stir in the tomato paste, taking care not to let it burn (thereby making it bitter). Pour in the veal stock and bring to a boil.

Reduce heat, cover, and simmer for 30 minutes. Season with salt, and sprinkle in the parsley and fennel leaves. Return the soup to a boil briefly, adjust the seasonings, reduce heat, and keep warm.

2. For the toasted bread, preheat the oven to 390–400⁰. Place the slices of bread on a baking sheet, drizzle with the olive oil, and toast for a few minutes until crisp.

3. Ladle the soup into a tureen. Remove the bread from the oven and layer on top. Sprinkle the bread with the grated cheese, parsley, and fennel leaves and serve right away.

Beet essence with duck ravioli

Soup cuisine at its finest — an elegant broth with a distinctive garnish: pasta, stuffed with duck breast and liver

Serves 4
For the broth:
5 teaspoons butter
⅔ cup onion, 2 garlic cloves, 4 cups beets, *1 cup carrots, ⅜ cup celery, ½ cup leeks, all diced*
¾ cup white wine
1 sprig each thyme and rosemary, 2 bay leaves
2 cloves, 5 allspice berries, 10 white peppercorns
For clarifying the essence:
14 oz chopped beef shin, 1¾ cups diced beets
1 garlic clove, ¼ cup celery, ½ cup leeks, all diced
5 egg whites
1 sprig each thyme and rosemary
For the ravioli dough:
¾ cup wheat flour
1 egg, 1 egg yolk, salt, water
For the stuffing:
3½ oz chilled, finely diced, skinned duck breast
1½ oz chilled, finely diced duck foie gras (liver)
⅛ cup finely chopped shallots, 1 teaspoon butter
generous pinch grated orange rind
¼ cup freshly squeezed orange juice, ⅓ cup cream
1 teaspoon thyme, salt, freshly ground white pepper
For the garnish:
parsley leaves

Melt the butter and sauté the onion and garlic until lightly browned. Add the beets, carrots, celery, and leeks, and sauté briefly. Pour in the wine and simmer. Add the herbs and spices and 11 cups of water; bring to a boil. Reduce heat; simmer for 1 hour. Remove from heat; let steep for 1 hour. Strain and cool completely. To clarify the essence, follow the photo sequence opposite. To make the ravioli, knead all the ingredients into a smooth dough. Form into a ball, wrap in plastic, and chill for 1 hour. For the stuffing, sauté the shallots in the butter until translucent. Stir in the orange rind and juice, reduce down to 1 tbsp, and cool. Purée the duck breast, livers, shallots, and cream; strain; and season with thyme, salt, and pepper. Roll out the very thin dough and cut into 1½-inch squares.

Place a little stuffing on each and fold into triangles, sealing the edges Boil the ravioli until they rise to the surface. Ladle the essence into bowls, add the ravioli, and garnish with parsley right before serving.

To clarify the essence, put the meat and vegetables through the coarse blade of a meat grinder.

Stir the meat, beets, garlic, celery, leeks, and egg whites together in a pot. Add the thyme and rosemary.

Pour in about 5 cups of the cooled beet broth and bring to a boil, stirring constantly.

As soon as a white scum forms and the meat rises to the top, reduce heat and simmer for 15 minutes.

Pour through a conical sieve lined with a piece of cheesecloth. Return to the pot and adjust the seasonings. Bring to a boil and skim off the fat. Keep hot.

Ribollita

A classic Tuscan dish: "reboiled" bean soup, flash-broiled with Parmesan

The idea that soups and stews taste better the following day is particularly true for *ribollita*. Originally, this soup was nothing more than an admittedly delicious way of using up leftovers. Once the soup was prepared, it was reheated again and again, thus becoming thicker and more tasty. In Tuscany, incidentally, instead of a piece of ham, they often like to add a ham bone to the soup as it cooks. If making this variation, before putting the soup in the oven, take out the ham bone, remove and dice the meat, and return it to the soup.

Serves 4–6

8½ oz dried white beans, 4 tablespoons olive oil
1 diced garlic clove, ⅔ cup diced white onion
5 oz piece of ham
1 small, dried chile pepper
2 thyme sprigs, 1 small rosemary sprig
1 cup carrots, diced into ¼-inch pieces
⅔ cup thinly sliced celery
¾ cup leeks, cut into thin rings

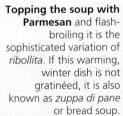

Topping the soup with Parmesan and flash-broiling it is the sophisticated variation of *ribollita*. If this warming, winter dish is not gratinéed, it is also known as *zuppa di pane* or bread soup.

5½ oz Swiss chard, sliced into ½-inch strips
salt, freshly ground pepper
You will also need:
4–6 slices toasted country bread (preferably from Tuscany)
10½ teaspoons freshly grated Parmesan

1. Place the beans in a bowl with enough cold water to cover and let soak overnight. The next day, pour off the water and drain well.

2. Heat half of the olive oil in a large pot and sauté the garlic and onion without letting them brown. Add the beans and the ham and pour in 9 cups of water; bring to a boil. Reduce heat and

add the chile pepper, thyme and rosemary sprigs. Simmer, covered, for about an hour. Keep warm.

3. Heat the remaining olive oil in a frying pan and sauté the carrots, celery, and leeks for 3–4 minutes, stirring continuously. Add the vegetables to the beans and ham and simmer for another 40 minutes. Add the Swiss chard to the soup last, and simmer for an additional 20–25 minutes.

4. Preheat the oven to broil. Remove the ham from the soup and cut into very small cubes. Set aside.

5. Finely purée half of the soup in a blender and return to the pot. Sprinkle in the cubed ham and season with salt and pepper.

6. Place the toasted bread slices in deep, ovenproof soup plates and sprinkle with half of the Parmesan. Ladle in the soup, sprinkle with the remaining cheese, and flash briefly in the oven to melt the cheese. Serve immediately.

Tuscan vegetable soup with beans and artichokes

This traditional *zuppa garmugia* is served with freshly toasted croutons

Brown or kidney beans, available both dry and in cans, are very well suited to soups and stews because of their hearty flavor. The dry beans take 1–2 hours to cook once they have been soaked. For very soft beans, extend the cooking time appropriately. Canned beans only need to be rinsed under cold water and added to the soup 10 minutes before the end of cooking time.

Serves 4

⅓ cup dry kidney beans
10½ oz small artichokes (without their stalks)
3 tablespoons olive oil, 4½ oz ground beef
⅓ cup diced, uncooked bacon
⅔ cup leeks, sliced diagonally into ¼-inch rounds
⅔ cup onion, sliced into thin rings
4½ cups beef or vegetable stock
8½ oz (unshelled weight) fresh, shelled peas (about 3½ oz shelled weight)
salt, freshly ground pepper

Some artichoke varieties, when young and tender, can be prepared and eaten whole. In Italy, they are even sold already cooked. Small, thorny artichokes are prepared like the large varieties.

For the croutons:

2 tablespoons olive oil, 1 garlic clove
2 slices white bread (crusts removed), cut into cubes

1. Place the beans in a bowl with enough cold water to cover and let soak overnight. The next day, pour off the water, rinse the beans well, and bring to a boil. Reduce heat and simmer for about 45 minutes. Drain well; set aside.

2. Prepare the artichokes: If necessary, strip off the small, tough leaves around the base of the stalk. Using kitchen scissors, remove the prickly tips of the leaves. Cut off the top portion — about one-third — evenly with a sharp knife. Quarter the artichokes; scoop out the fibrous, inedible choke with a teaspoon and discard. Set aside the remainder.

3. Heat the olive oil in a pot and brown the ground beef, breaking it up as it cooks. Add the bacon and continue to brown. Add the leeks and onion and sauté them until translucent. Pour in the stock and bring to a boil. Add the beans and the reserved artichokes, reduce heat, and simmer for 10 minutes. Add the peas, season with salt and pepper, and simmer the soup for another 10 minutes. Keep warm.

4. For the croutons, heat the olive oil in a frying pan. Squeeze the garlic through a press into the pan. Add the bread cubes and fry until golden brown and crunchy. Ladle the hot soup into bowls, sprinkle the croutons on top, and serve at once.

Silversides are every bit as delicate as they look. Because of this, they can be cooked with almost no further preparation. Scaling, boning, and even gutting are unnecessary.

Vegetable soup with silversides

This light, summer soup is best served with *fettunta*, a toasted garlic bread

Nearly every visitor to the Mediterranean has eaten them at some time, the tiny silversides that also go by the name of "sandsmelts." They are usually pan-fried or deep-fried whole, covered in a crispy batter, or marinated before frying. If you are able to come by this delicate fish, take advantage of the opportunity to make the vegetable soup presented here. *Fettunta* can be prepared in a number of ways. For the simplest variation, slices of toasted white bread are rubbed with garlic and drizzled with fruity, green olive oil; but the bread can also be flavored with herbs. For instance, 2 finely chopped garlic cloves and 1 teaspoon parsley, spread on a freshly toasted slice of ciabatta or country bread, drizzled with 2 tablespoons olive oil, seasoned with salt and freshly ground pepper, and served piping hot, tastes incredible. Instead of parsley alone, a mixture of parsley, sage, oregano, and thyme could also be used.

Fettunta is a popular Tuscan appetizer — primarily because it is so quick and easy to prepare, but also because it is delicious.

Fish and vegetables — a classic combination in most of the world's cuisines, not only highly recommended pan-fried or baked, but also in soups.

Serves 4
10½ oz silversides
8½ oz tomatoes, blanched, skinned, seeded, and diced (reserve the seeds)
2 tablespoons olive oil
⅓ cup shallots, sliced into thin rings; 1 finely chopped garlic clove
⅔ cup leeks, sliced into thin rings
⅜ cup thinly sliced celery
¾ cup thinly sliced carrots
½ cup white wine, 3½ cups fish stock
1 teaspoon lemon juice
salt, freshly ground pepper
For the garnish:
1 tablespoon chopped tarragon, tarragon sprigs

1. Carefully place the silversides in a large colander, rinse under cold water, drain well, and refrigerate.

2. Strain the tomato seeds through a fine-mesh sieve, reserving the juices; set aside.

3. Heat the olive oil in a pot and sauté the shallots and garlic until translucent. Add the leeks, celery, and carrots, and sauté briefly.

4. Add the wine and simmer over medium heat for 5 minutes. Stir in the diced tomatoes and tomato juice, pour in the fish stock, reduce heat,

and simmer for another 8 minutes or so. Season with lemon juice, salt, and pepper.

5. Add the silversides, and simmer over low heat for 4–5 minutes. Adjust the seasonings, ladle into bowls, garnish with the chopped tarragon and tarragon sprigs, and serve.

In the Mediterranean, fish and shellfish are usually trawled. Only small boats that specialize in catching premium fish use a longline (long fishing line with attached hooks).

Minestra di verdura con rana pescatrice

An exquisite puréed vegetable soup with monkfish, langoustines, and shavings of mild cheese

If a vegetable soup usually brings to mind a thick, clear broth with different vegetables (such as celery, carrots, leeks, and potatoes) rounded out with white beans, noodles, bacon, or some other meat, this delectable recipe will come as a surprise. This prize soup tastes even better if homemade vegetable stock (made from fresh produce) is used.

The different varieties of Caciotta are produced in central Italy, chiefly from cow's or sheep's milk, and less frequently from a mixture of cow's, sheep's, and goat's milk. For this recipe, an aged Caciotta with a hard interior is required. The flavor of this cheese is pleasantly mild and sweet.

Monkfish is virtually boneless, aside from the spinal column. It is also very firm, and therefore ideally suited for this soup, along with the langoustine tails.

Serves 4
1¼ lb tomatoes, blanched, skinned, seeded, and diced (save the seeds)
8 tablespoons olive oil
¾ cup finely chopped onion
2 finely chopped garlic cloves
2 cups diced yellow peppers

12½ oz mealy potatoes, cut into small cubes
1 tablespoon tomato paste
4½ cups vegetable stock
salt, freshly ground pepper
1¼ lb skinned monkfish, 4 langoustines
salt, freshly ground pepper
For the garnish:
small basil leaves
2 tablespoons freshly grated, aged Caciotta cheese

1. Press the tomato seeds through a sieve and reserve the juice.

2. Heat half of the olive oil in a pot and sauté the onion and garlic without letting them brown. Add the diced tomatoes, peppers, and potatoes, and braise for 5 minutes. Stir in the tomato paste and sauté for 2 minutes. Pour in the reserved tomato juice and the vegetable stock, season with salt and pepper, and bring to a boil. Reduce heat, and simmer for 25 minutes. Blend until smooth with a handheld blender, adjust the seasonings, and keep warm.

3. Wash the monkfish under cold water, then pat dry and remove any remaining bits of skin. Cut the monkfish into ½–¾-inch medallions; the

spinal column can be easily cut through with a heavy knife. Twist off the langoustine tails from the heads and devein. Set aside the seafood.

4. Heat the remaining olive oil in a frying pan. Season the monkfish medallions with salt and pepper, and brown for about 2 minutes on each side. Add the langoustines and sauté for 1 minute.

5. Ladle the soup into heated soup plates. Add the monkfish medallions and the langoustine tails. Serve garnished with the basil leaves and the grated cheese.

Onion soup

With a hearty garnish, *cipollata* is an ideal soup for wintry days

Vinschgauer Fladen, a German flat bread made of rye and wheat flours and flavored with fennel, aniseed, or caraway, goes very well with this hearty soup (if you can find it) — it also helps with the digestion. The slices of bread can be sprinkled with grated Parmesan, instead of Emmental or Bergkäse (mountain cheese).

Serves 4

1⅓ lb tomatoes, blanched, skinned, seeded, and diced (save the seeds)
⅔ cup diced, uncooked bacon
4 tablespoons olive oil, 5 teaspoons butter
4⅛ cups onion, sliced into thin rings; 1 teaspoon sugar
4½ cups vegetable or chicken stock
salt, coarsely ground black pepper
For the garnish:
1 Vinschgauer loaf (about 5½ oz), sliced ½-inch thick
2–3 tablespoons extra virgin olive oil, 2 eggs
salt, freshly ground pepper
2½ teaspoons butter
¾ cup grated hard cheese (Emmental, Bergkäse)
1 tablespoon chopped herbs (parsley, basil)

1. Press the tomato seeds through a sieve and reserve the juice.

2. Sauté the bacon in a pot. Add the oil, butter, and onion, sprinkle in the sugar, and simmer over low to medium heat for 15 minutes, until golden brown.

3. Pour in the stock and reserved tomato juice and add the diced tomatoes. Season with salt and pepper and bring to a boil. Reduce heat and simmer for 15–20 minutes. If necessary, pour in a little more stock and adjust the seasonings. Keep warm.

4. For the garnish, preheat the oven to 390–400⁰. Place the bread slices on a baking sheet, drizzle with a little olive oil, and toast until golden brown. Remove and set aside.

5. Whisk the eggs in a bowl and season with salt and pepper. Melt the butter in a frying pan and pour in the eggs. As soon as they begin to set, stir continuously, pushing toward the center, until they are uniformly creamy but still moist and shiny.

6. Ladle the soup into warmed soup plates. Layer on a slice of toasted bread, sprinkle with the cheese, and top with the scrambled egg. Garnish with coarsely ground pepper and the chopped herbs before serving.

Goulash soup

Gulyás leves — a classic of Hungarian cuisine

Contrary to any popular prejudices about cheap, canned soups, this dish, when made from scratch using fresh ingredients, is a true delicacy. Slow simmering in the oven is essential for its thick, creamy consistency and appetizing taste. Goulash soup is ideal for preparing in larger quantities to freeze and reheat as needed.

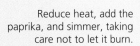

Melt the butter in an ovenproof pot and sauté the onion until translucent.

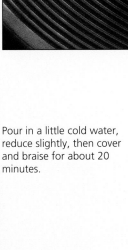

Gulyás leves can be served as an appetizer, a first-course soup, or as the main course, depending on portion size.

Reduce heat, add the paprika, and simmer, taking care not to let it burn.

Pour in a little cold water, reduce slightly, then cover and braise for about 20 minutes.

Stir in the tomato paste, add the vinegar, and simmer.

Add the potatoes and stir into the meat mixture.

Sprinkle the cubed beef with salt and add to the pot. Season with garlic, caraway seeds, and marjoram.

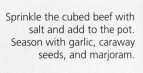

Add plenty of water and simmer until the potatoes begin to disintegrate.

Serves 4

1⅓ lb pure beef (chuck or round)
7½ teaspoons butter
1⅔ cups finely chopped onion
1 tablespoon Hungarian paprika
1 tablespoon tomato paste
1 tablespoon vinegar
salt
1 finely chopped garlic clove
generous pinch ground caraway seeds
½ teaspoon marjoram
7 oz mealy potatoes, cut into ½-inch cubes

To make the beef easier to slice, it is advisable to put it in the freezer shortly before preparation. Remove the slightly frozen meat and cut it first into ½-inch-thick slices, then into small cubes. Set aside. Prepare the goulash soup as shown in the picture sequence. Preheat the oven to 300⁰.

Cook the soup on the stove, covered, until the potatoes begin to disintegrate. Transfer the pot to the oven and simmer gently, uncovered, for several hours. Serve and enjoy.

Dingač is one of the best red wines from Croatia. It is made in legally protected areas in Dalmatia from ripe — in some cases dry — *Plavač* grapes. Served as an accompaniment, its full-bodied sweetness, coupled with its fresh bouquet, takes the edge off the spiciness of the soup.

Hot-pepper soup
A fiery stew, rounded out with fresh oregano and basil

As in all the countries of the former Yugoslavia, sitting down to a meal in Croatia is still a communal event. Accordingly, the soup is traditionally placed in the center of the table, and then ladled into the bowls of those gathered round — an example you may wish to follow to be truly authentic.

The finest-tasting oregano, sharp and spicy, flourishes in the limestone areas of Croatia. Like many other herbs that can be found in the garden, it is used frequently for seasoning hearty stews.

Croatia's hearty soups, though not as famous as her meat dishes, are every bit as tasty, as evidenced by this peppery soup.

Serves 4
½ cup dried red kidney beans
1 garlic clove
salt
2 tablespoons vegetable oil
1⅔ lb beef (chuck), cut into ½-inch cubes
1¼ cup onion, sliced into thin rings
2⅔ cups green bell peppers, cut into ½-inch cubes
10 black olives, pitted and halved
1 lb tomatoes, blanched, skinned, seeded, and diced
4½ cups meat stock
2 thinly sliced hot green peppers (about ½ oz)
1 tablespoon pickled green peppercorns
You will also need:
1 teaspoon coarsely chopped oregano
a few basil leaves

1. Rinse the beans under cold water, then place in a bowl with enough cold water to cover and let soak overnight. The next day, pour off the water,

place the beans in a sieve or colander, and drain well. Set aside.

2. Peel the garlic, place on a flat surface or use a mortar and pestle, sprinkle with some salt, and crush to a smooth paste.

3. Heat the vegetable oil in a pot and brown the beef on all sides. Add the onion and garlic and sauté briefly. Add the bell peppers, olives, tomatoes, and the drained beans. Pour in the meat stock and add the hot peppers and peppercorns.

4. Bring to a boil. Reduce heat and simmer for about 90 minutes. If the soup becomes too thick, add a little more stock. Adjust the seasonings. Sprinkle with oregano and basil, ladle into individual soup bowls, and serve.

Each step in the manufacture of paprika — from the washing to the chopping, drying, and grinding of the peppers, to the interim storage of the powder in sacks — is stringently monitored. The paprika shown here was produced in Hungary, but Romania also boasts a modest number of paprika mills.

Colorful sweet-pepper soup

The influence of Hungarian cuisine on Romanian cooking is unmistakable in this dish

In the following recipe, a variety of bell peppers (of different colors) is recommended to achieve a beautiful, multihued effect. Since the color of the peppers has only a slight influence on the flavor of the soup, they may be mixed in whatever proportions desired. They may also be cut into rings or strips, depending on the effect to be created. If fresh rosemary is not available, the dried version may be substituted.

Romano and crème fraîche provide a cool garnishment to this mildly spicy soup.

Serves 4
1 tablespoon olive oil
⅞ cup finely chopped onion
1 finely chopped garlic clove
10–12 finely chopped fresh rosemary leaves
¼ cup red cherry peppers, sliced into rings
4 cups bell peppers (of mixed colors), sliced into rings or cut into strips
3½ cups vegetable stock
3 teaspoons Hungarian paprika
1 teaspoon hot paprika, salt
For the garnish:
7 oz Romano, diced into small cubes
1–2 tablespoons heavy cream blended with small dash of buttermilk (crème fraîche)

1. Heat the olive oil in a pot and sauté the onion and garlic until translucent, stirring occasionally. Add the rosemary and continue to sauté. Add the cherry and bell peppers and sauté these briefly, stirring from time to time.

2. Pour in the vegetable stock and bring to a boil. Season with the Hungarian paprika and hot paprika. Cover, and simmer over moderate heat until the peppers are *al dente* (about 6 minutes). Season with salt.

3. Ladle the soup into warmed bowls and garnish each with a few cubes of cheese and a dollop of crème fraîche.

Tarator with a fine garnish

Trout-mousse-stuffed cucumbers lend a touch of sophistication to this substantial summer soup

In Bulgaria, *tarator* is served on hot summer evenings as a pleasantly refreshing soup. The variation suggested here calls for Kirby cucumbers. These cucumbers, which weigh from 3½–8½ oz each and grow up to 7 inches in length, are widely grown in the United States, Israel, and Turkey. Should this variety be unavailable, an English or hothouse cucumber may be substituted.

Serves 4
For the cucumber filling:
3½ oz trout fillet, cut into cubes; salt
freshly ground white pepper
generous pinch yellow mustard powder
dash lemon juice
½ cup ice-cold cream
1 teaspoon chopped dill
2 Kirby cucumbers (about 5½ oz each)
For the soup:
1¼ lb Kirby cucumbers
salt, 3 garlic cloves
14 oz plain yogurt
freshly ground white pepper
1 tablespoon olive oil

This cucumber soup is served ice cold as a first course. It is traditionally accompanied by schnapps, also chilled, which is intended to prepare the palate (and the stomach) for the dishes to follow.

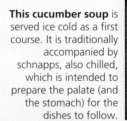

Use an apple corer to hollow out the cucumbers. Spoon the filling into a decorating bag with a round, No. 2 tip and squeeze it into the cucumbers, then replace their "lids." Butter two pieces of aluminum foil large enough to cover, and wrap one cucumber tightly in each, twisting the ends of the foil to seal. Pierce the cucumbers through the foil at regular intervals with a needle.

Yogurt is often featured in the national cuisines of the Balkans — particularly those of Bulgaria, Greece, and Turkey.

1 tablespoon chopped dill
1 tablespoon chopped mint
You will also need:
a little butter for greasing the foil
crushed ice, 7½ teaspoons chopped walnuts

First prepare the filling for the cucumbers: Sprinkle the trout cubes with salt, pepper, and mustard powder, and drizzle with lemon juice. Cover and marinate in the refrigerator until well chilled, or put in the freezer for 10 minutes. Purée the trout cubes with the cream in a blender until smooth. Press the mixture through a fine-mesh sieve into a bowl. Stir in the dill, adjust the seasonings, and return the filling to the refrigerator. Wash and pat dry the two cucumbers, cutting off both ends to be used later as "lids." Preheat the oven to 350⁰. Proceed as shown in the picture sequence opposite.

Place the foil-wrapped cucumbers on a baking sheet and bake for 25 minutes or so, turning them from time to time. Remove from the oven and let cool in the foil. For the soup, wash and peel the cucumbers, halve them lengthwise, and scoop out the seeds with a teaspoon. Slice the cucumber halves into julienne strips, place in a bowl, sprinkle with salt, and let sit for 30 minutes; then gently squeeze the cucumber strips to expel the excess liquid. Set aside. Peel the garlic and squeeze through a press into a bowl. Stir in the yogurt and season with pepper. Stir in the olive oil, dill, and mint. Mix in the cucumber strips and refrigerate the soup for 1 hour to allow the flavors to mingle. Remove the stuffed cucumbers from the foil and slice into rounds. Ladle the soup into bowls and add a little crushed ice to each. Garnish with the stuffed cucumber rounds and walnuts and serve nice and cold.

Lemons are grown almost everywhere in Greece and — so it seems to the visitor, at any rate — are served with almost every dish, usually in thick wedges, for squeezing individually over one's plate.

Lemon soup

Kotosoupa avgolemono (lemon-chicken sauce): A light chicken soup, enhanced with a mixture of egg and lemon juice

Avgolemono, the egg and lemon juice mixture often used in Greece, is the basis of many soups in its native country, whether meat, fish, or poultry based. It is also often used to bind sauces. The lemon juice adds a pleasantly tart, fresh note. If an even sharper taste is preferred, the amount of lemon juice for this recipe can be increased by half, that is, up to ¾ cup.

Serves 4
1 boiling chicken, giblets removed (about 3 lb)
salt, ¾ cup coarsely chopped carrots
⅔ cup coarsely chopped leeks
½ cup coarsely chopped celery, ⅔ cup coarsely chopped onion
freshly ground white pepper
For the egg–lemon juice mixture (avgolemono):
2 eggs, 2 egg yolks
½ cup lemon juice
You will also need:
¾ cup cooked long-grain rice (optional)
small peppermint leaves

Wash the chicken inside and out under cold water and drain well. Bring to a boil in a large pot with 6½ cups of water. Add 1 teaspoon salt, reduce heat, and simmer for 30 minutes, repeatedly skimming off any scum that rises to the surface. Add the carrots, leeks, celery, and onion and simmer for another 1½ hours over low heat. Remove from heat, take out the chicken, drain well, and let cool slightly. Set aside. Line a conical sieve with a piece of cheesecloth and strain the liquid into a pot. Season with salt and pepper, then skim off the fat, either by drawing a paper towel over the surface to absorb the fat, or

by chilling and then skimming off the congealed fat with a slotted spoon. There should be about 4½ cups of broth remaining. Reheat and keep warm. Prepare the avgolemono sauce as shown in the picture sequence below. Slowly add the egg-lemon-broth mixture to the hot chicken broth, stirring constantly. Keep warm over low heat and stir until slightly creamy, but do not allow to boil. Remove the skin from the chicken, separate the meat from the bones, and cut into bite-sized pieces. Divide the meat among 4 soup plates and add the cooked long-grain rice (if desired). Ladle in the soup and serve garnished with mint leaves.

Whisk the eggs and egg yolks together in a bowl, until foamy.

Gradually add the lemon juice to the egg mixture, stirring constantly.

Slowly add about one-third of the hot broth, stirring continuously to prevent the egg yolk from curdling.

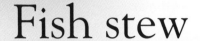

Fish stew

With whole gurnard cut into chunks, and plenty of vegetables

Sometimes a soup, sometimes a thick stew — fish recipes of this sort are popular throughout Greece. The fish and vegetables may also be removed from the broth and served after the latter as a main course.

Serves 4
2 gutted gurnards, (about 1¼ lb each)
For the court bouillon:
1 cup white wine
⅔ cup onion, 1 garlic clove, ½ cup each carrots and leeks, ½ cup celery, all coarsely chopped
2 bay leaves, 2 thyme sprigs
5 white peppercorns, coarse sea salt
For the vegetable mixture:
2 tablespoons olive oil
½ cup finely chopped onion
14 oz potatoes, cut into ½-inch cubes
salt, freshly ground pepper

Greek fishermen catch their fish every day. This is why one can enjoy excellent seafood dishes on the coast, sometimes even in small, quaint tavernas.

The world-famous bouillabaisse Provençale, it has been said, is derived from Greek fish stews such as this. With or without this illustrious descendant, the Greek variant is sheer poetry on a plate.

1 cup thinly sliced carrots, ⅔ cup thinly sliced leeks
⅔ cup thinly sliced celery
4½ oz dolma peppers, diced into ½-inch cubes
1 small sliced Charleston pepper (about 1 oz)
14 oz tomatoes, blanched, skinned, seeded, and diced
3½ oz olives
½ lemon, sliced into rounds
For the garnish:
1 tablespoon chopped herbs (parsley, thyme)

1. Wash the fish thoroughly and drain well. Cut off the fins and discard; slice the remainder

crosswise into 1½-inch-thick chunks. Cover and refrigerate.

2. To make the court bouillon, pour ½ cup of water and the wine into a pot. Add the onion, garlic, carrots, leeks, celery, bay leaves, thyme, and peppercorns. Season with salt and bring to a boil. Reduce heat and simmer for 20 minutes.

3. To make the vegetable mixture, heat the olive oil in a large pot and sauté the onion without letting it brown. Add the potatoes, pour in enough water to cover, and bring to a boil.

Reduce heat and simmer for 5 minutes. Season with salt and pepper. Add the carrots, leeks, celery, and peppers and simmer for another 10 minutes. Add the tomatoes and simmer for 5 minutes more. If necessary, add a little water.

4. Add the fish chunks to the court bouillon, simmer for about 10 minutes, and remove. Remove the court bouillon from heat, line a conical sieve with cheesecloth, and strain; then pour it over the vegetable mixture. Carefully add the fish, olives, and lemon slices and heat through; garnish with the herbs and serve immediately.

Bean soup

Rustic, hearty, and uncomplicated: *fassolia soupa* with white beans

If the beans are skinned after cooking — time consuming, but perhaps worth it — they are much more digestible.

Serves 4
10½ oz large, dried white beans
14 oz tomatoes, blanched, skinned, seeded, and diced (save the seeds)
2 tablespoons olive oil
¾ cup finely chopped onion
1 finely chopped garlic clove
1 cup finely diced carrots
⅔ cup finely diced celeriac
¾ cup leeks, sliced into thin rings
4½ cups chicken stock
salt, freshly ground pepper
For the garnish:
1 tablespoon chopped herbs (parsley, oregano)

1. Place the beans in a bowl with enough cold water to cover and let soak overnight. The next day, drain off the water, pour the beans into a sieve or colander, and rinse well under cold water. Transfer the beans to a pot and bring to a boil with about 6½ cups of water; reduce heat and simmer for about 1 hour, until soft. Pour off the water, then rinse under cold water and skin the beans. Set aside.

2. Press the tomato seeds through a sieve, reserving the juice. Set aside.

3. Heat the olive oil in a pot and sauté the onion and garlic without letting them brown. Add the carrots, celeriac, and leeks and sauté briefly. Pour in the chicken stock and bring to a boil. Reduce heat and simmer for 15 minutes. Stir in the diced tomatoes and the reserved juice, and simmer for another 10 minutes. Add the skinned beans, season with salt and pepper, and simmer for a few minutes more. Garnish with the herbs and serve at once.

Many towns in Greece, such as Hydra, pictured here, still have a rustic character in some areas. Likewise, some of the most popular Greek dishes are also rather rustic in nature — like the bean soup on this page.

Tarhana çorbasi

An "instant soup" with a difference, prepared from a special dried, yogurt-flour mixture

To prepare *tarhana* oneself would be a several-day-long undertaking; fortunately, it is available ready-made from Turkish food stores. The dry, powdery, semolina-like mixture — a specialty originally from central Anatolia — is traditionally prepared by kneading wheat flour and yogurt into a dough with finely diced vegetables such as tomatoes, sweet peppers, and onions, as well as yeast and meat broth. The dough is then placed in a linen sack and hung up in a warm, well-ventilated spot. Over a period of three days or so, the dough must be knocked down hard in the sack each time it rises. It is then removed and broken up into little lumps that are exposed to full sun until absolutely all liquid has evaporated. Crumbled or ground, the powder then becomes a base for the potent *tarhana çorbasi*, which is still sometimes served for breakfast in the Turkish countryside.

Serves 4
3 oz tarhana
3 tablespoons olive oil
8½ oz ground lamb
¾ cup finely chopped onion, 2 finely chopped garlic cloves
14 oz tomatoes, blanched, skinned, seeded, and diced into ¼-inch cubes
4½ teaspoons tomato paste
4½ cups lamb stock
salt, freshly ground pepper
1 teaspoon Hungarian paprika
For the garnish:
1 tablespoon chopped parsley

1. Place the *tarhana* in a bowl and soak in a little water for 20 minutes.

2. Heat the olive oil in a pot and sauté the lamb until well browned all over. Add the onion and garlic and sauté briefly. Add the tomatoes and stir in the tomato paste. Pour in the lamb stock and bring to a boil. Add the *tarhana*, stirring until dissolved.

3. Reduce heat and simmer for 15 minutes. Season with salt, pepper, and paprika. Pour the soup into a tureen, garnish with the parsley, and serve right away.

Lentil soup with leeks and fish

The garnishes in this recipe lend a touch of class to the humble legume, which otherwise belongs in the realm of everyday cooking

Lentil soup — prepared in various ways — is one of the classic dishes of the eastern Mediterranean. In Turkish cooking, soups made primarily from the small, red lentil — the quick-cooking legume that usually disintegrates almost immediately, providing a lovely creaminess — are known and popular, but this kind of soup also tastes very good made with green lentils. Not completely an authentic Turkish recipe, but quite delicate nonetheless, is a version using dark-green, French Puy lentils, which harmonize beautifully with the fish fillet.

Serves 4
1 cup green lentils
4 tablespoons olive oil
2 cups finely chopped onion
2 finely chopped garlic cloves
1 teaspoon finely grated fresh turmeric root
1/2 teaspoon ground cumin
3 1/2–4 1/2 cups vegetable stock
salt, freshly ground pepper
1 tablespoon lemon juice

Instead of John Dory, this lentil soup can be topped with sea bream or whiting fillets.

For the leeks:
1 tablespoon olive oil
2/3 cup leeks, 1 red chile pepper, both sliced thin; salt
For the fish:
4 John Dory fillets (3–4 oz each)
salt, freshly ground pepper
2 tablespoons olive oil, 5 teaspoons butter
For the garnish:
cilantro leaves

Cumin seed, one of the spices most typical of Near and Middle Eastern, as well as North African cuisines, comes in both lighter and darker varieties.

1. Place the lentils in a sieve or colander and rinse under cold water. Transfer to a pot with enough cold water to cover and bring to a boil.

Reduce heat and simmer for 10 minutes. Remove from heat, and drain well. Set aside.

2. Heat the olive oil in a pot and sauté the onion and garlic for 2–3 minutes without letting them brown. Add the turmeric root and cumin and sauté for another 2 minutes. Sprinkle in the lentils. Pour in the vegetable stock, season with salt and pepper, and bring to a boil. Reduce heat and simmer for 40 minutes.

3. Remove from heat, and purée until smooth. Return to heat, add the lemon juice, and adjust the seasonings.

4. To prepare the leeks, heat the olive oil in a frying pan and sauté the leeks and chile pepper for 5 minutes over low heat. Season with salt and keep warm.

5. To prepare the fish, halve them lengthwise and season with salt and pepper. Heat the olive oil and butter together in a frying pan and brown the fillets for about 2 minutes on each side.

6. Ladle the soup into bowls, add the fish fillets, and arrange the leeks and pepper on top. Garnish with cilantro leaves and serve.

Harira

A nourishing lamb soup with legumes and rice — in Morocco, most popular after the Ramadan fasts

Serves 4

1½ oz dried garbanzo beans, ½ cup brown lentils
5¼ cups lamb stock, ¼ cup long-grain rice
2 teaspoons flour, 7½ teaspoons butter, 1 tablespoon vegetable oil
8½ oz lamb fillet, sliced ¼-inch thick
1¼ cups diced onion, 2 diced garlic cloves, ½ oz diced fresh ginger
1 teaspoon ground cinnamon
½ teaspoon ground turmeric
14 oz tomatoes, blanched, skinned, seeded, and diced into ½-inch cubes
1 tablespoon each chopped parsley and cilantro, salt freshly ground pepper, 1 egg and 1 tablespoon lemon juice whisked together
For the garnish:
chopped cilantro

1. Rinse the garbanzo beans and lentils separately under cold water then place in separate bowls, cover with cold water and soak overnight. The following day, pour off the water, rinse in fresh water, and drain well. Set aside.

2. Transfer the beans to a pot, add 2¼ cups of water, and bring to a boil. Reduce heat and simmer, covered, for 40 minutes. Drain and set aside.

3. In another pot, heat half the lamb stock. Add the lentils and rice, and simmer over low heat for 10 minutes. Mix the flour with 1 tablespoon of water, stir until a smooth paste is formed, and add to the lentils and rice; stir well.

4. Heat the butter and oil together in a large frying pan and brown the lamb thoroughly. Add the onion, garlic, and ginger, and sauté for 3 minutes. Add the cinnamon and turmeric and sauté for another 2 minutes. Pour in the remaining lamb stock and simmer for 10 minutes.

5. Stir in the tomatoes, beans, lentil-rice mixture, parsley, and cilantro. Season with salt and pepper and simmer for another 10 minutes.

6. Stir the egg and lemon juice mixture into the soup. Garnish with cilantro and serve.

Everywhere in the medina — the old part of Marrakesh full of interesting nooks and crannies — there are small shops and stands where people can purchase their staple foods.

Red lentil soup

With a duet of garnishes: pan-fried shrimp, and a juicy vegetable mixture

Many everyday Egyptian dishes have a legume base: for example, the ubiquitous *ful*, a bean stew with lots of olive oil, served lukewarm. A frequently used favorite is lentils, especially the small red or yellow varieties. The deceptively simple lentil soup recipe on this page is a true classic; its seasonings and garnishes give it an unexpected zing. Those who prefer a purely vegetarian dish can substitute crisp, golden-brown croutons for the shrimp.

Serves 4
5¼ cups beef stock
1¼ cups red lentils, rinsed and drained
1 small onion studded with 1 bay leaf and 2 whole cloves
2 whole, peeled garlic cloves
salt, freshly ground white pepper
1 generous pinch ground cumin
For the onion-tomato mixture:
¼ cup butter

A spice seller at a Cairo market offers artistically mounded wares for sale — enough for 1,001 culinary delights.

A garnish of pan-fried shrimp is unusual in this traditional Egyptian soup, but they round out the flavor perfectly.

⅔ cup finely chopped onion
7 oz tomatoes, blanched, skinned, seeded, and finely diced
salt, freshly ground white pepper
For the shrimp garnish:
¼ cup butter
8 medium-sized raw shrimp tails, shelled
salt, freshly ground white pepper
You will also need:
2 tablespoons chopped parsley

1. Bring the beef stock to a boil in a large pot. Add the lentils, studded onion, and garlic. Season with salt, pepper, and cumin. Reduce heat, cover,

and simmer for 20 minutes, making sure the lentils do not boil over.

2. In the meantime, make the onion-tomato mixture: Melt the butter in a frying pan and sauté the onion without letting it brown. Add the tomatoes and sauté for 5 minutes, then season with salt and pepper. Remove from heat and set aside.

3. Remove the studded onion from the pot and purée the stock with a handheld blender. Adjust the seasonings and keep warm.

4. For the shrimp garnish, melt the butter in a frying pan and sauté the shrimp tails for 2 minutes on each side. Season with salt and pepper.

5. Ladle the soup into warmed soup plates. Divide the onion-tomato mixture among the bowls and add the shrimp. Sprinkle with parsley and serve right away.

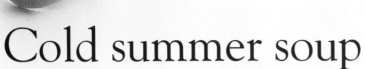

Cold summer soup

Made from *chana dal* (as the split garbanzo beans are called in India), tomatoes, and cucumbers

The different regional cuisines of India are known for their imaginative approach to vegetarian cooking. Various legumes (known in Hindi as *dal*), chief among them lentils and garbanzo beans, provide a major source of protein and are thus a staple item for any menu. When buying the ingredients for this recipe, make sure to buy real *chana dal*, since this recipe will not work with whole, dried garbanzo beans.

Serves 4

12½ oz chana dal (split garbanzo beans)
½ oz finely grated fresh turmeric root
½ teaspoon cumin seeds
1 green chile pepper, cut into thin strips; juice of ½ lime
salt, freshly ground pepper
½ cup scallions, sliced into thin rings
8 oz tomatoes, blanched, skinned, seeded, and diced into ¼-inch pieces
1⅓ cups cucumbers, peeled, seeded, and diced into ¼-inch pieces
You will also need:
½ cup yogurt
1 tablespoon chopped cilantro leaves

1. Soak the *chana dal* in cold water for 1½ hours, then pour into a colander, rinse thoroughly under cold water, and drain well.

2. Bring 9 cups of water to a boil in a large pot. Add the *chana dal* and turmeric and simmer, covered, over low heat for about an hour and 20 minutes. Make sure the contents of the pot do not boil over.

3. Remove from heat, ladle off all the liquid above the *chana dal* (which will be sitting on the bottom), and set aside. Purée the remaining contents in a blender, transfer to a bowl, and stir in enough of the reserved liquid to yield a creamy soup. Set aside.

4. Dry-roast the cumin seeds in a heavy pan until they release their fragrance, then grind them to a powder with a mortar and pestle. Stir the cumin, chile pepper, and lime juice into the soup; season with salt and pepper; and refrigerate.

5. Ladle the chilled soup into bowls; add the scallions, tomatoes, and cucumbers; and top with a dollop of yogurt. Just before serving, stir in the cilantro leaves.

Different varieties of chile peppers are on display at this Indian market. The hot and spicy pods — originally from Latin America — are red when ripe; green chile peppers are harvested before ripening. **Caution — after working with chile peppers, do not rub your eyes, as the residue from your fingers will cause a painful burning sensation.**

At the food stalls of Asia, such as here in Chiang Mai, rice snacks are available throughout the day as a delicious way of quelling between-meal hunger pangs.

Rice soup with shrimp
This kind of rice soup is served for breakfast in many Thai households

Khao tom gung, as this soup is called in Thailand, can be prepared with chicken stock, or just plain water, instead of fish stock.

Serves 4
For the garlic oil (prepared a few weeks in advance):
6 garlic cloves
2¼ cups vegetable oil
For the *nam prik* sauce:
4 finely chopped garlic cloves
¼ cup finely chopped shallots
1 tablespoon shrimp paste (trasi)
¼ teaspoon salt
1 tablespoon sugar
8 red Thai chile peppers, seeded and halved lengthwise
juice of 2 limes
few spoonfuls chicken broth
For the soup:
7 oz cleaned squid
9 cups fish stock
½ teaspoon salt
⅞ cup Thai long-grain rice (e.g., Jasmine rice)
7 oz medium-sized shrimp tails, peeled and deveined
4 Chinese pork sausages, cut into 1½-inch-long sections
4 eggs
For the garnish:
½ cup scallions, cut crosswise into thin strips
1 tablespoon cilantro leaves

1. To make the garlic oil, peel and halve the garlic cloves, place in a bottle, and add the vegetable oil. Seal the bottle well and let stand at room temperature for 2–3 weeks.

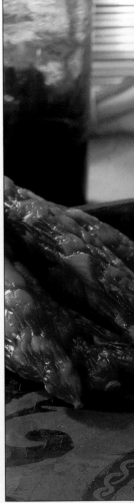

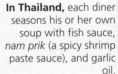

In Thailand, each diner seasons his or her own soup with fish sauce, *nam prik* (a spicy shrimp paste sauce), and garlic oil.

The *nam prik* sauce gives a certain edge to the soup without adulterating its essentially mild taste.

2. For the *nam prik* sauce, grind the garlic and shallots to a paste in a mortar with the shrimp paste, salt, and sugar. Blend the chile peppers and lime juice to a fine purée in a food processor or blender. Add the garlic-shrimp paste, mixing together only briefly. Thin the sauce as desired with chicken broth and set aside.

3. For the soup, skin the squid by holding firmly in one hand while pulling off the skin with the other. Pull the tentacles out of the body sac and cut off from the head just above the eyes so that they remain joined by a narrow ring. Be careful not to pierce the ink sac. Grasp the ring from underneath in the center, pop out the beak with your index finger, and cut it out. Then remove the transparent cartilage from the body sac. Carefully wash the tentacles and mantle (body), leaving the former whole and cutting the latter into ¼-inch-wide rings. Set aside.

4. Bring the fish stock to a boil with the salt. Add the long-grain rice and simmer, covered, over low heat for 20 minutes. Add the squid rings and tentacles, shrimp, and sausage during the final 10 minutes of cooking time.

5. Ladle the soup into bowls and crack open an egg into each. Garnish with the scallions and cilantro leaves and serve. Pass around the garlic oil, *nam prik* sauce, and (if desired) fish sauce, so each bowl can be seasoned separately.

The charmed life of a duck: waddling along between rice fields, quacking and pecking at plentiful food. No wonder the meat of these birds is both low in fat and very tasty.

Duck wonton soup
Deep-fried wontons make a crisp contrast for tender meat in a spicy broth

Most of the ingredients in this recipe are easy to obtain, though it might be a little harder to find the cilantro root. This should be no problem for herb gardeners, however, who can grow their own at home. Alternatively, parsley root may be substituted.

Serves 4
For the soup:
½ oven-ready duck (about 1¾ lb)
1 oz lemongrass, sliced into thin rounds
1 oz finely chopped cilantro root
2 lime leaves, 1 red chile pepper
1 tablespoon vegetable oil, ⅔ cup finely chopped shallots
2 finely chopped garlic cloves
1 tablespoon chopped cilantro leaves
¼ teaspoon ground coriander
salt, freshly ground pepper
4 tablespoons fish sauce, 1 7–10-oz can water chestnuts
For the wontons:
¼ cup finely chopped scallions
1 finely chopped red chile pepper
½ oz finely chopped fresh galangal, 1 finely chopped garlic clove

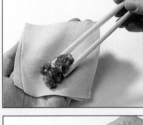

Use 2 of the wonton wrappers at a time, one on top of the other. Place a little filling on the bottom third of the wonton and roll up two-thirds of the way.

Brush both ends of the filled wonton with a little egg white and press tightly together.

Pull the two tips of the wonton skins apart. Cover with a damp cloth and set aside.

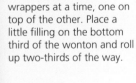

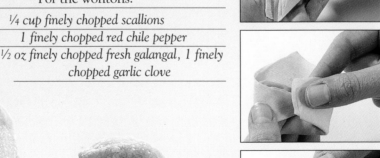

juice and grated rind of ½ lime
1 teaspoon chopped cilantro leaves, 1 tablespoon light soy sauce
salt, freshly ground pepper, 1 egg yolk
16 wonton skins, 1 egg white
You will also need:
vegetable oil for deep-frying
For the garnish:
⅓ cup scallions, sliced into thin rings

For the soup, wash the duck under cold water and drain well. Set aside 4 oz of skinless duck meat for the wonton filling. Place the remaining duck, lemongrass, cilantro root, lime leaves, and chile pepper in a large pot with enough cold water to cover and bring to a boil. Reduce heat and simmer for about an hour, until the meat is tender. In the meantime, heat the vegetable oil

and sauté the shallots and garlic until lightly browned. Stir in the cilantro leaves, coriander, salt, pepper, and fish sauce, and sauté. Add this mixture to the soup 15 minutes before the end of cooking time and the water chestnuts 5 minutes later. Remove the duck from the soup, separate the meat from the bones, cut into bite-sized pieces, and return to the soup. To make the wonton filling, chop the reserved duck meat very fine. Carefully mix together the scallions, chile pepper, galangal, and garlic with the duck meat, lime juice and rind, cilantro leaves, soy sauce, salt, pepper, and egg yolk. Proceed as shown in the picture sequence opposite. Heat the vegetable oil to 350⁰ and deep-fry the wontons until golden brown. Reheat the soup. Adjust the seasonings, ladle into small bowls, add 2 wontons to each bowl, and garnish with the scallions. Serve immediately.

Lemongrass and lime leaves give the broth its distinctive flavor; Galangal suffuses the wonton filling. For a slightly more substantial soup, add a little cooked, flavored Thai rice as a garnish.

Bamboo shoot soup with crispy fish

— and that special something, thanks to a homemade roasted spice mixture

Serves 4
For the crispy fish:
1⅓ lb snapper fillet (halibut or catfish may be used), cut into 4 pieces
salt, freshly ground pepper
For the soup:
about 2¼ cups vegetable oil for frying
2 tablespoons peanut oil
¼ cup thinly sliced fresh ginger, ½ cup sliced shallots
2 thinly sliced garlic cloves, 2 chile peppers, cut in half
2 stalks citronella or lemongrass (about 1 oz), cut into 1-inch pieces
2 cardamom pods

Thailand's waters offer fishermen an abundance of marine delicacies — among them deliciously edible fish such as those from the snapper family.

3¼ cups fish stock, 3–4 tablespoons fish sauce
½ oz tamarind pulp mixed with ½ cup hot water
salt, freshly ground pepper
14 oz canned bamboo shoots, drained and sliced
7 oz tomatoes, blanched, skinned, seeded, and diced
You will also need:
½ cup cooked long-grain rice, a few cilantro leaves

1. Season the fillet pieces with salt and pepper, and refrigerate.

2. For the soup, heat the peanut oil and stir-fry the ginger, shallots, garlic, chile peppers, citronella or lemongrass, and cardamom pods. Let cool, then grind to a powder with a mortar and pestle.

3. Bring the fish stock to a boil. Stir in the prepared spice mixture, reduce heat, and simmer for 10–15 minutes. Add the fish sauce and tamarind pulp and and stir. Remove from heat and strain through a fine-mesh sieve. Re-heat, and season with salt and pepper. Stir in the bamboo shoots and tomatoes.

4. Heat the vegetable oil to 350⁰ and stir-fry the fish pieces one at a time, until crispy. Drain.

5. Ladle into 4 bowls. Add the fish, together with the rice and cilantro leaves, and serve.

Eggplant is not only fried in Laotian cooking, as in this recipe, but is also boiled and used as a thickening agent for braising, or mixed with fish to make a spicy paste.

Noodle soup with fish and pork

A Laotian national dish, typical in its imaginative combination of simple ingredients

In Laos, soups such as this one — which is known as *khao phoune* — are served for breakfast. The dish is usually prepared by placing noodles into a large serving bowl, topping them with fresh vegetables and herbs, and ladling in some broth. Of course, the soup may also be served at other times of day.

Serves 4
3 coarsely chopped garlic cloves, 1 cup coarsely chopped onion
1¼ lb pork (shoulder cut)
10 oz red snapper fillet, 3 tablespoons peanut oil
½ oz finely chopped fresh ginger
3 finely chopped red chile peppers
4½ cups coconut milk
½ cup ground roasted peanuts
salt, 1 tablespoon fish sauce, 4 oz soybean sprouts
5 oz small Asian eggplant, sliced into rounds
¾ cup green beans, cut diagonally into thin slices
8 oz slightly underripe mango, peeled, pitted, and diced into ½-inch pieces
⅔ cup cucumbers, peeled and sliced into thin rounds
1 cup daikon, peeled and diced into ¼-inch pieces
⅔ cup scallions, sliced into rounds; ¾ cup rice vermicelli
For the garnish:
8–10 small mint leaves

1. Bring the garlic, onion, and pork to a boil in a pot with 3¼ cups of water. Reduce heat and simmer for about 1½ hours. (Add more water if necessary to make sure that the pork remains covered at all times.) Remove the pork and let cool; set aside. Add the snapper fillet and simmer for about 4–5 minutes, until cooked. Carefully remove the fillet and set aside. Remove from heat and strain through a fine-mesh sieve — there should be about 2¼ cups of broth remaining. Set aside.

2. Heat 1 tablespoon of peanut oil in a large wok and sauté the ginger and chile peppers until lightly browned. Add the coconut milk and simmer; stir in the peanuts and bring to a boil. Reduce heat and simmer for 5 minutes. Season with salt and fish sauce. Pour in the reserved broth and simmer for another 5 minutes. Keep warm.

3. Dice the pork into ¼-inch pieces and break up the snapper fillet up into bite-sized pieces. Set aside.

4. Blanch the soybean sprouts briefly in boiling water. Drain well and set aside. Heat the remaining 2 tablespoons of peanut oil in a frying pan and sauté the eggplant slices on both sides until crisp. Remove, drain on paper towels, and set aside.

5. Simmer the green beans in the stock for 5 minutes, then add the sprouts, mango, cucumbers, daikon, pork, and snapper and simmer for 1 minute. Add the eggplant and scallions last. Adjust the seasonings with salt and fish sauce. Cook the rice vermicelli for 3–4 minutes in boiling, salted water and drain well. Divide the vermicelli among 4 soup bowls, ladle in the soup, and serve garnished with mint leaves.

Noodle soup with meat and seafood

Hearty and substantial — brimming with pork belly, spiny lobster, shrimp, squid, and chicken

Nuoc mam, Vietnam's ubiquitous sauce made from salted fish, also lends additional spiciness to this soup. Just how much spiciness is up to the individual, since the sauce, which can be purchased ready-made in Asian food stores, is put on the table for each person to use as desired.

Serves 4
1 cooked spiny lobster tail (about 12½–14 oz)
5½ oz uncooked pork belly, salt
5½ oz skinned, boned chicken breast
5½ oz medium-sized shrimp tails
1 squid (about 5½ oz)
3½ cups chicken stock
1 red chile pepper, halved; ⅓ cup finely chopped scallions
freshly ground pepper
3½ oz thin Asian egg noodles
You will also need:
2 tablespoons peanut oil
½ cup shallots, sliced into rings
1 tablespoon chopped cilantro leaves
fish sauce (nuoc mam)

In many Asian countries, long, thin noodles — like the "longevity noodles" in this soup — symbolize a long life. Whatever its effect on the life span, eating such a delicious soup at least guarantees living well!

1. Crack open the lobster tail and remove the meat, keeping it as intact as possible. Remove the intestine at the tail end and carefully pull out from the other side. Cut the meat crosswise into even pieces. Cover and refrigerate.

2. Place the pork belly in a pot with about 1 cup of water, season with salt, and bring to a boil.

Reduce heat and simmer for 20 minutes. Add the chicken breast and simmer for another 10–15 minutes; both the pork and chicken should remain covered with water. Keep warm.

3. Peel the shrimp tails, devein, and set aside. Wash and skin the squid. Pull out the tentacles and cut off just above the eyes so that they remain joined by a narrow ring. Grasp this ring from below in the center, pop out the beak, and cut out. Remove the cartilage from the body sac. Wash the body and the tentacles thoroughly. Cut the body into thin strips; leave the tentacles whole.

4. Remove the pork belly and the chicken breast from the stock and set aside. Remove from heat and pour the stock through a fine-mesh sieve. Pour the strained stock back into the pot, add the chicken stock and chile pepper, and bring to a boil.

5. Stir half of the scallions into the soup. Add the squid strips and tentacles. Simmer for 5 minutes, then add the shrimp and simmer for 3 minutes at a low boil.

6. Cut the pork belly into bite-sized pieces and slice the chicken breast. Heat both, together with

the lobster meat, in the soup. Season with salt and pepper and keep warm.

7. Cook the noodles for about 5 minutes in boiling, salted water and drain well. Heat the peanut oil in a frying pan and sauté the shallots until golden brown and crisp. Remove with a slotted spoon and drain well on paper towels.

8. Divide the cooked noodles among 4 soup bowls. Ladle the hot soup with the pork and chicken meat and the seafood over the noodles. Top with the remaining scallions, fried shallots, and the chopped cilantro. Serve with *nuoc mam*.

Beef broth with noodles and water chestnuts

A clear soup that can be seasoned at the table with *nuoc cham* and fish sauce

Water chestnuts have their name in common with native chestnuts, and even taste similar. Botanically speaking, though, they are a member of the sedge family. The water chestnut is found in West Africa, Madagascar, and India, but chiefly throughout East Asia, where it is particularly popular. In the West, the tubers with the firm, creamy-colored interior are usually sold ready to use in cans. If, however, fresh water chestnuts are available, by all means try out this tasty soup, known as *bo bun hue* in Vietnamese.

Serves 4
For the broth:
¼ cup sliced fresh ginger, 1 quartered small–medium onion
1½ lb beef brisket, 10½ oz beef shin, with the bone
1 piece tangerine peel
4 whole anise pods, salt
5½ oz fresh water chestnuts
3½ oz fresh soybean sprouts
8½ oz mee (Chinese egg noodles)
⅔ cup scallions, sliced into thin rings
For the nuoc cham sauce:
4 teaspoons lime juice
¼ cup fish sauce
4½ teaspoons brown sugar, 1 red chile pepper, sliced into rings
2 tablespoons chopped roasted peanuts
¼ cup grated carrots
You will also need:
1 tablespoon cilantro leaves, fish sauce (nuoc mam)

1. In a large pot, bring 9 cups of water to a boil with the ginger, onion, beef brisket and beef shin, tangerine peel, and anise. Reduce heat, season with salt, and simmer for about 2½ hours.

2. Meanwhile, prepare the *nuoc cham* sauce: Stir together the lime juice, fish sauce, brown sugar, and ¼ cup of water until the sugar has dissolved, then add the chile pepper, peanuts, and carrots. Set aside.

3. Wash the water chestnuts thoroughly, discarding any that look yellowish or withered. Peel the remaining chestnuts with a sharp knife as you would an apple, removing the tough stalk end. Slice into rounds and set aside.

4. Sort through the soybean sprouts, discarding any that are discolored, then rinse and blanch for ½ minute; drain well and set aside. Remove the beef from the broth and cut into thin slices. Remove the broth from heat and pour through a fine-mesh sieve. Boil the noodles in lightly salted water for about 8 minutes, then drain well and set aside.

5. Return the broth to heat and bring to a boil. Add the water chestnuts and simmer for 5 minutes. Adjust the seasonings.

6. Divide the noodles among 4 soup plates, top with the sliced beef, and sprinkle over the scallions and soybean sprouts. Ladle in the broth with the water chestnuts. Sprinkle over the cilantro leaves and serve with *nuoc cham* sauce and fish sauce.

Tomato egg drop soup

Light, slightly tart, and refreshing — this soup brings to mind hot summer days

Not just French, but Chinese gastronomy as well, has left its mark on the cuisine of Vietnam. This Vietnamese tomato egg drop soup, therefore, is probably inspired by Chinese culinary methods. The recipe comes from the south of the country, where fruit and vegetables flourish in great variety. Lime leaves, which simmer in the chicken broth, give the soup an especially refreshing twist. It is also seasoned with *nuoc mam*, the ever-present Vietnamese fish sauce.

Serves 4
2 tablespoons peanut oil
⅔ cup shallots, sliced into rings; 1 tablespoon sugar
1⅓ lb tomatoes, blanched, skinned, seeded, and cut into ¼-inch strips
5¼ cups chicken stock
¾ oz coarsely diced fresh ginger
3 lime leaves, salt, freshly ground pepper
2–3 tablespoons fish sauce (nuoc mam)
3 eggs, ½ cup scallions, sliced into thin rings
For the garnish:
a few cilantro leaves

1. Heat the peanut oil in a pot and sauté the shallots until translucent. Sprinkle in the sugar and allow to caramelize. Add the tomatoes, cover, and braise briefly, then pour in the chicken stock. Add the ginger and lime leaves, and bring to a boil. Reduce heat and simmer for 20 minutes. Season with salt, pepper, and fish sauce.

2. Remove the ginger and the lime leaves at the end of 20 minutes and discard.

3. Ladle off 1 cup of soup and pour into a small pot; heat to just below boiling. Beat the eggs and slowly trickle into the hot soup. After 30 seconds, gently stir with a fork — this creates the "egg drops" — and simmer briefly.

4. Bring the remaining soup to a boil once more. Using a slotted spoon, transfer the "egg drops" from the broth to the soup, discarding the broth after removing the egg drops. Simmer together for 1 minute, stirring carefully. Add the scallions; season to taste with fish sauce, salt, and pepper; and garnish with cilantro leaves. Serve immediately.

Light and airy "egg drops" lend a special touch to this delicious soup. To keep it clear, ladle off a little broth and simmer the "egg drops" in this, rather than stirring the egg directly into the soup. After removing the "egg drops," it is recommended that this broth be used in a different recipe or discarded, since it would inevitably make the soup cloudy if added back in.

Cream of corn soup

This soup gets its special texture from a blend of whole and puréed corn kernels

Sweet corn, a form of Indian corn or maize (which originated in Central and South America and has been known for millennia), was first cultivated in this country in the 17th century. Since the Second World War it has been grown increasingly throughout the world, including Vietnam, where it forms the basis of this soup.

Sweet corn is ripe when the "silk" emerging from the top of the cob has turned brown. The kernels will then be light to dark yellow, plump, and smooth.

Serves 4
5 ears of fresh sweet corn (about 7½ oz each), salt
1⅓ lb chicken legs
¾ cup chopped carrots, ½ cup chopped onion
¼ cup chopped celery, ½ cup chopped leeks
2 tablespoons peanut oil
2 finely chopped garlic cloves
1 cup sliced shallots, ½ cup sliced scallions
2 tablespoons Vietnamese fish sauce
freshly ground pepper
2 teaspoons cornstarch dissolved in 1 tablespoon water

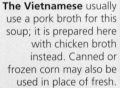

The Vietnamese usually use a pork broth for this soup; it is prepared here with chicken broth instead. Canned or frozen corn may also be used in place of fresh.

For the garnish:
1 tablespoon vap ca, *cut into strips*

Vap ca is an herb from Vietnam. Its heart-shaped leaves are edged with a narrow band of red. Fresh and lemony tasting, it is used in traditional Vietnamese cooking to enhance soups and salads.

1. Husk the sweet corn, remove the silk, and boil for 25 minutes in lightly salted water. Remove and let cool. Cut off the kernels with a sharp knife, reserving the kernels from one cob. Purée the remaining kernels and press through a fine sieve. Set aside.

2. Wash the chicken legs under cold water. Bring about 5 cups of water to a boil, add the carrots, onion, celery, leeks, and chicken legs, and

simmer over low heat for 20–25 minutes. Remove the chicken legs, let cool slightly, and skin them. Separate the meat from the bones and cut into small pieces; set aside. Remove the broth from heat, strain, and set aside.

3. Heat the peanut oil in a wok and stir-fry the garlic, shallots, and scallions for about 1 minute. Add the chicken meat and reserved corn kernels, and stir-fry for another 3–4 minutes. Add the fish sauce, simmer, and season with salt and pepper.

4. Bring 4½ cups of the broth to a boil and carefully stir in the puréed corn. (Any leftover broth can be frozen.) Thicken with the dissolved cornstarch and return to a boil. Add the contents of the wok and simmer for 5 minutes. Adjust the seasonings carefully with salt, pepper, and fish sauce, (the latter can be very salty). Ladle the soup into heated bowls, garnish with the *vap ca*, and serve. This soup can be enhanced even more by adding a beaten egg after thickening with cornstarch and boiling for one minute (stirring constantly), before adding the chicken and the corn kernels.

Asparagus soup with rice and fried fish

In this recipe, the stock is made from the asparagus peelings, so none of the flavor of this wonderful vegetable is lost

Red snapper — one of the most popular food fish in Asia — is perfect in this soup, but grouper or sea bass can also be used. If you do not wish to scale and gut the fish yourself, have it done at the fish market. To minimize dealing with the bones, the fillets (with the skin on; frying makes it appetizingly crisp) can be cut diagonally into strips and prepared as indicated in the recipe.

Serves 4
1 red snapper fillet (about 12½ oz)
14 oz thinly peeled white asparagus, cut into 1½-inch sections (save the peelings), salt
2 small red chile peppers, halved; ½ oz thinly sliced fresh galangal root
2 thinly sliced garlic cloves, ¾ oz thinly sliced lemongrass
3½ oz Asian short-grain rice
1½ oz snow peas, cut diagonally into ½-inch pieces
3 tablespoons oyster sauce, 4 tablespoons light soy sauce
freshly ground pepper, 4 tablespoons vegetable oil
For the garnish:
1 tablespoon chopped Vietnamese cilantro (rau ram)
¼ cup scallions, sliced into thin rings

1. To gut and scale the snapper, grip firmly at the tail end with a cloth and cut off the fins in the direction of the head. Scrape off the scales, also working toward the head. Slit open the belly lengthwise with a sharp knife, starting at the anus. Remove the intestines and cut off the head. Wash thoroughly inside and out under cold water and pat dry. Cut the cleaned fillet crosswise into 1-inch-thick slices. Cover and refrigerate.

2. Wash the asparagus peelings and boil in 6½ cups of water for 15 minutes. Measure off about 5 cups of this stock and set aside. (Any leftover stock can be frozen and used in other recipes.)

3. Salt the asparagus stock very sparingly and bring to a boil with the chile peppers, galangal root, garlic, lemongrass, and rice. Reduce heat and simmer for 5 minutes. Add the asparagus sections and simmer for another 5 minutes, then add the snow peas and simmer for 3–4 minutes more. Add the oyster sauce and soy sauce. Keep warm.

4. Season the snapper with salt and pepper. Heat the vegetable oil in a wok or frying pan, and stir-fry the snapper thoroughly for about 3 minutes, until crispy. Arrange in 4 small bowls and ladle in the soup. Garnish with the *rau ram* and scallions, and serve.

Crisp-fried fish and crunchy vegetables in a well-seasoned asparagus broth — each component of this soup is actually a delicacy in itself.

A shark fin, dried and skinned. The individual muscle fibers separate from one another during the lengthy drying process, making an interesting pattern more reminiscent of a plant part than a fish fin.

Shark fin soup
This delicacy requires some time to prepare

In China, dried shark fins are an expensive delicacy. In the Middle Kingdom, they are used in countless varieties of soup (with, for example, duck and Hunan ham), or served braised. In order to turn the dried fins — which are as tough as leather — into an exotic morsel, a long process of soaking, cleaning, parboiling, and final cooking in a spicy broth is necessary. It is said of this soup, therefore, that it takes three days to prepare but only three minutes to eat. It is almost impossible to recreate authentically this famous Chinese dish in the West, but for those who do not balk at the challenge, the following basic recipe is recommended.

A soup for festive occasions — served in a suitably aristocratic tureen. The variation of shark fin soup shown here was prepared with sliced abalone and Chinese broccoli.

Chinese traders import dried shark fins from all over the world. The dorsal fins of almost all varieties of shark are sold, but those of a few species — for example, the blacktip shark — are especially prized. The dried fins are parboiled by specialized companies in a time-consuming process, then prepared and redried before being sold.

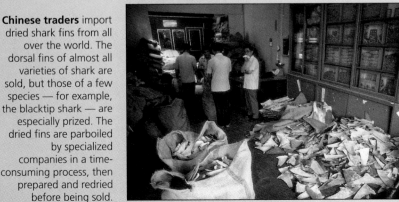

Serves 6–8
3½ oz dried shark fins
9 cups chicken stock, 4 scallions
½ oz fresh ginger, sliced into rounds
1 oz dried mushrooms
2 tablespoons oil, 8½ oz chicken breast, cut into strips
1 tablespoon rice wine, 2 tablespoons soy sauce
1 tablespoon red rice vinegar, ½ teaspoon each sugar and salt
3½ oz canned sliced bamboo shoots
3 tablespoons cornstarch, dissolved in cold water

1. Soak the shark fins for 24 hours. Drain and wash thoroughly several times, in order to remove

all impurities and any remaining bits of skin.

2. Place the fins in a pot with fresh water and bring to a boil. Simmer for 2 hours, changing the water several times during this period. Remove and pat dry.

3. Return the fins to the pot and bring to a boil with 3¼ cups of chicken stock. Add the scallions and the ginger and return to a boil. Reduce heat and simmer for 15 minutes. Remove from heat. Take out the scallions and ginger and discard. Set aside the broth with the shark fins.

4. In the meantime, soak the dried mushrooms for about 20 minutes. Then squeeze lightly, cut out the hard stalks, and quarter the caps. Set aside.

5. Heat the oil in a large wok and stir-fry the chicken. Remove and set aside. Pour in the remaining chicken stock and the broth with the fins and bring to a boil. Add the mushrooms and season with rice wine, soy sauce, rice vinegar, sugar, and salt. Simmer for 15–20 minutes, then add back the chicken and stir in the bamboo shoots.

6. Add the dissolved cornstarch and thicken the soup. Adjust the seasonings and serve piping hot.

Chicken soup with coconut milk

It is important to heat the coconut milk very slowly so that it combines with the broth to produce a creamy texture

Serves 4
For the chicken broth:
1 prepared chicken (about 3 lb)
10½ oz Hunan ham, cut into 2 pieces; ½ cup leeks, sliced into rings
1 oz thinly sliced fresh ginger
1 small piece dried tangerine peel
2 tablespoons rice wine
1 teaspoon salt
For the soup:
⅓ cup Asian long-grain rice, salt
1 stalk lemongrass, sliced into thin rings
2 lime leaves, sliced into thin strips
3 green chile peppers, sliced into thin rings
⅓ cup celery, cut into 2-inch-long pieces
grated rind and juice of 1 lime
⅔ cup scallions, sliced into thin rings
1½ teaspoons sugar, freshly grated pepper
2¼ cups coconut milk
For the garnish:
4 teaspoons Chinese leeks, sliced into small rings

To make the chicken broth, wash the chicken inside and out under cold water; drain well, and transfer to a large pot. Proceed as shown in the picture sequence opposite. Remove the chicken from the broth and set aside. Measure off 2¼ cups of broth for the soup; the remainder may be frozen for use in other recipes. To make the soup, cook the rice in lightly salted water for 15–18 minutes; drain well and set aside. Bring the chicken broth to a boil with the lemongrass and lime leaves, then reduce heat and simmer for 10 minutes. Add the chile peppers, celery, lime rind, lime juice, and scallions and simmer for another 2–3 minutes. Season with sugar, salt, and pepper. Stir in the coconut milk and heat slowly. Skin the chicken. Separate the meat from the bones, cut

into bite-sized pieces, and arrange in 4 soup bowls with the rice. Ladle in the hot soup and serve garnished with the leeks.

Place the ham slices in the pot with the chicken, pour in 3½ qt of cold water, and bring to a boil.

Simmer the broth for about 2 hours over low heat, repeatedly skimming off the scum that rises to the surface.

Add the leeks, ginger, tangerine peel, rice wine, and salt. Simmer over low heat for another hour.

The broth will be ready after a total of 3 hours. Remove from heat and strain through a sieve lined with cheesecloth. There should be about 9 cups of broth.

Place three tofu slices side by side. Dust the first one sparingly with cornstarch, then spread the shrimp mixture all the way to the edges and sprinkle with more cornstarch.

Dashi with vegetables and shrimp

It is remarkable how such simple ingredients can be so elegantly presented

This recipe uses many ingredients essential to Japanese cooking: *kombu* and bonito flakes (the components of the dashi broth), as well as tofu and soy sauce. *Mirin* is a sweet rice wine that is not drunk, but used exclusively for cooking. Made from *mochi-gome*, a short-grained, starchy rice, it has an alcohol content of 13–22 percent.

Serves 4
For the shrimp mixture:
7 oz raw, shelled shrimp tails
2 teaspoons finely grated fresh ginger
salt, freshly ground black pepper
1 tablespoon mirin, 1 egg yolk
½ tablespoon cornstarch dissolved in a little water
13½ oz tofu, cut into 6 slices ½-inch thick
1 tablespoon cornstarch
For the dashi broth:
½–¾ oz kombu (seaweed), 1 oz bonito flakes
5 tablespoons soy sauce, 3 tablespoons mirin, salt
You will also need:
2 pieces of gauze (about 10 x 10 inches)
2 cups shelled peas, 5½ oz spinach
1 cup carrots, sliced into 2-inch-long julienne strips
For the garnish:
nasturtium flowers

Remove and coarsely chop the shrimp meat. Purée together the shrimp, ginger, salt, pepper, *mirin*, egg yolk, and the dissolved cornstarch. Press through a fine-mesh sieve and refrigerate. For the dashi broth, wipe the white powder off the *kombu* with a damp cloth and boil in 4½ cups

Place a second slice of tofu on top of the first and proceed as with the first slice. Top off with the third slice, which is left plain; press together slightly and wrap in a piece of gauze. Repeat with the remaining three slices.

of water. Reduce heat and simmer for 10–15 minutes. When bubbles rise to the surface, check to see if the seaweed is soft; if not, simmer for another minute. Remove the *kombu* and discard. Add ½ cup of cold water, sprinkle in the bonito flakes, and return to a boil. Remove from heat and wait until the fish flakes sink to the bottom. Strain through a piece of cheesecloth and season with soy sauce, *mirin*, and salt. Set aside. Layer the tofu slices and shrimp mixture into two "sandwiches," as described in the picture sequence, wrap in gauze, and steam for 15 minutes. Reheat the broth, add the steamed tofu blocks, and simmer for 10 minutes. Then remove, unwrap from the gauze, cut crosswise into ½-inch slices, and set aside. Boil the peas separately for 5 minutes, remove, and set aside. Add the spinach, blanch for 1 minute, remove, and drain. Simmer the carrots in the broth for 4 minutes; add back the spinach and peas, and adjust the seasonings. Ladle the broth into bowls, add the tofu slices, garnish with a nasturtium flower, and serve.

Braised celery goes well with this broth. To make it, sauté 2 cups of thinly sliced celery for 1 minute in 2 tablespoons of vegetable oil. Add 2 tablespoons of rice wine, cover, and braise until the liquid has evaporated. Season with a little sugar, 3 tablespoons of soy sauce, some salt, and freshly ground pepper, and sprinkle with toasted sesame seeds.

Vegetable-scallop soup

Exquisitely prepared, using chicken stock rather than a dashi broth

In Japan (likewise in the West), clear soups are a popular way to begin a meal. This particular broth — which, like most Japanese soups, is quick and easy to prepare — has a beguiling garnish of crunchy vegetables, making a distinctive counterpoint for the tender scallops and their coral (roe). Japanese fan scallops (whose reddish-brown and ivory-colored sides symbolize in Japan the sun and the moon, respectively) would most likely be used for the garnish. Here, the equally delicate deep-sea or bay scallops can be used. Substituting one variety for another is not only permissible from a Japanese culinary standpoint, it is also part of following their traditional recipes, which frequently list a whole range of alternative ingredients that can be used to prepare the dish. Thus, this soup can also be garnished with shrimp instead of scallops.

Scallop meat with crunchy vegetables in a mildly spicy broth: a delicious combination to please Eastern and Western palates alike.

Serves 4
4 bay scallops
½ oz dried mushrooms, soaked in a little cold water
4½ cups chicken stock
2 tablespoons light soy sauce
1 tablespoon sake
salt, freshly ground pepper
¾ cup carrots, cut into julienne strips
1½ oz snow peas, diagonally sliced
For the garnish:
1 tablespoon chopped parsley

1. Wash and scrub the scallops thoroughly under cold water. To open them, hold each one firmly in a cloth, flat side up. Insert the tip of a sharp, sturdy knife between the two shells, slice through the muscle on the inside of the flat shell, and lift off the top shell. Loosen the scallop at the gray edge of the meat and remove. Pull off the gray edge from the white muscle (noisette) and the reddish-orange roe (coral). (Though not used here, it makes an excellent ingredient for a fish stock.) Carefully separate the noisette and the coral.

2. Dip both the noisette and coral in hot water for several seconds, remove, cool slightly, and cut into strips about ¼ inch wide by 1½ inches long. Set aside.

3. Gently squeeze out the mushrooms, cut into thin strips, and set aside.

4. Bring the chicken stock to a boil in a pot and season with soy sauce, sake, salt, and pepper. Reduce heat, add the carrots, and simmer for 5 minutes. Stir in the snow peas and mushrooms and simmer for another 5 minutes.

5. Add the scallop noisette and coral last and simmer over low heat for 2–3 minutes. Adjust the seasonings, ladle the soup into 4 individual serving bowls, and serve garnished with parsley.

Kombu and *katsuo-bushi*: Seaweed and bonito flakes, both dried, are the main ingredients in a classic dashi broth with its fresh sea flavor, which serves as the basis of many soups in Japan.

Vegetable soup with crabmeat balls

With delicate garnishes that perfectly complement the broth in terms of flavor — that's how the Japanese love their soups

Serves 4
For the crabmeat balls:
¼ oz dried mushrooms
7 oz diced white fish fillet (e.g., cod)
1 egg white, 1 tablespoon cornstarch dissolved in 1 tablespoon water
1 tablespoon sake, 1 tablespoon mirin (rice wine)
salt, fresh ground white pepper
3 oz diced crabmeat
For the dashi broth:
¾ oz kombu, 1 oz bonito flakes
1 tablespoon soy sauce, salt
freshly ground pepper (sansho)
For the soup:
¾ cup green beans, cut diagonally into ¼-inch pieces
¾ cup julienned carrots, ½ oz sliced ginger
1½ oz shiitake mushrooms, halved or quartered
1 tablespoon cornstarch dissolved in 1 tablespoon water
1½ oz corn salad (mâche)

1. To make the crabmeat balls, soak the mushrooms in lukewarm water for 30 minutes. Squeeze out the mushrooms, finely chop, and set aside.

2. Purée the fish fillet with the egg white, dissolved cornstarch, sake, and *mirin*. Press through a fine-mesh sieve into a bowl, and season with salt and pepper. Mix in the crabmeat and mushrooms, cover, and refrigerate for two hours.

3. To make the dashi broth, rub the white powder off the *kombu* leaves with a damp cloth. Bring 4½ cups of water to a boil with the seaweed, then reduce heat and simmer for 10–15 minutes. As soon as bubbles rise to the surface, check with your fingernail to see whether the seaweed is soft; if not, simmer for 1–2 minutes more. Remove from heat, take out the *kombu* and discard. Add ½ cup of cold water. Stir in the bonito flakes and reheat to boiling, then remove from heat and wait until the fish flakes have fallen to the bottom. Strain through a sieve lined with cheesecloth and set aside.

4. Form the crabmeat-fish mixture into 12 small balls. Boil briefly in lightly salted water, reduce heat, and simmer for about 8 minutes, until done.

5. Reheat the broth, season with soy sauce, salt, and pepper, and bring to a boil. Reduce heat, add the green beans and carrots, and simmer for 5 minutes. Add the ginger and mushrooms and simmer for another 3 minutes. Add the dissolved cornstarch, let thicken, and return to a boil. Remove the crabmeat balls from the pot with a slotted spoon, drain well, and transfer to the soup. Add the mâche and simmer for 1 more minute. Ladle into bowls and serve.

Miso soup

With sautéed pork, vegetables, and *shichimi*, the famous Japanese, seven-spice mixture

In Japan, seasoning pastes made from fermented grains, soybeans, and sea salt are known as miso, and are sold in special miso stores. Depending on their age and composition, these pastes can vary greatly in terms of taste and texture, and production of miso is a science in itself. Miso is highly esteemed for its substantial protein and vitamin B_{12} content.

Serves 4
For the *shichimi* spice mixture:
½ teaspoon linseed, 1 teaspoon sesame seeds
½ teaspoon each dried orange peel and poppy seeds
2 small, dried chile peppers
1 teaspoon ao-nori (dried seaweed flakes)
sansho (Japanese pepper)
For the dashi broth:
½–¾ oz kombu (seaweed), 1 oz bonito flakes
For the soup:
2 tablespoons vegetable oil
4 oz thinly sliced boneless pork, cut diagonally into 1½-inch strips
¾ cup carrots and 3½ oz white asparagus, both sliced lengthwise into 1½-inch strips
1 oz thinly sliced fresh shiitake mushroom caps
1½ oz canned bamboo shoots
⅓ cup scallions, finely sliced on the diagonal
1 oz barley (mugi) miso, mixed to a smooth paste with a little cold water, salt

Miso soups are among the most popular of all soups in Japan. Enriched with a little pork and some vegetables, they make a very tasty dish, especially when enhanced with a pinch of *shichimi* powder.

Shichimi — also known as "seven-spice mixture" — is one of a few spice mixtures that are common to Japanese cooking.

1. First, make the *shichimi* spice mixture: Grind the linseed, sesame seeds, orange peel, poppy seeds, chile peppers, *ao-nori*, and pepper to a fine powder using a mortar and pestle. Set aside.

2. To make the dashi broth, rub the white powder off the *kombu* leaves with a damp cloth. Bring 4½ cups of water to a boil with the

seaweed, and simmer for 10–15 minutes. When bubbles rise to the surface, check to see whether the *kombu* is soft; if not, simmer for another minute. Remove from heat, take out the *kombu*, and discard. Add about ½ cup of cold water. Reheat and stir in the bonito flakes. As soon as the broth begins to boil, remove from heat and wait until the bonito flakes sink to the bottom. Then, strain through a sieve lined with cheesecloth and set aside.

3. For the soup, heat the vegetable oil in a large pot and sauté the pork until lightly browned. Add the carrots and sauté for 2 minutes. Mix in the

asparagus and mushrooms and sauté briefly. Pour in the dashi broth and simmer for 5 minutes. Stir in the bamboo shoots and scallions just before the end of simmering.

4. Stir in the barley miso paste, making sure it does not boil (thereby losing its nutrients). Season with salt and pepper and ladle into bowls. Sprinkle a little *shichimi* powder on top, and serve.

Mussels in chicken broth

A very delicate dish with Asian seasonings — sake, soy sauce, and lemongrass

The combination of shellfish and chicken broth is very common in Australian cuisine, having been exposed to Asian influences for some time. It only requires one taste of this soup to realize that these two ingredients blend together very well. To make about 3½ qt of chicken broth, you'll need a boiling chicken weighing about 5½ lb and 2¼ lb of veal bones. These are slowly simmered with 20 peppercorns, 2 garlic cloves, an onion studded with 4 whole cloves, and a bouquet garni in 4½ qt of water.

New Zealand mussels, easily recognizable by the characteristic green rim of their shells, are especially large.

For this mussel soup, using homemade chicken broth is recommended, as the flavor is better than that of canned.

Serves 4
2¾ lb New Zealand green-lipped mussels
4½ cups chicken broth (prepared as above, or canned)
1 piece lemongrass (about 4 inches long), halved lengthwise; 1 red chile pepper
1 tablespoon fish sauce, 2 tablespoons light soy sauce
2 tablespoons sake (rice wine)
1¼ cup carrots, sliced into thin, 2-inch-long pieces
⅞ cup celery, sliced into thin, 2-inch-long pieces
3 oz chopped canned bamboo shoots, salt
For the garnish:
1 tablespoon chopped Chinese chives

1. Scrub the mussels thoroughly under cold water to remove any sand or residue. Using your fingers, completely remove the beards and discard. Discard any mussels that are already open, as they could be spoiled. Set aside the remainder.

2. Pour the chicken broth into a wok or large frying pan. Add the lemongrass and chile pepper, (whole) to the broth and bring to a boil. Reduce heat slightly, and boil down to about 3½ cups. Season with fish sauce, soy sauce, and sake.

3. Add the carrots and celery and simmer for 5 minutes, stirring occasionally. Add the mussels and simmer over medium to high heat for 5–6 minutes, until they have opened. Discard any mussels that have not opened. Reduce heat, add the bamboo shoots, and simmer for another minute. Season to taste with salt.

4. Ladle the soup into bowls and garnish with the Chinese chives before serving.

Clam chowder
A delicious seafood recipe with smoked bacon and corn — somewhere between a soup and a stew in consistency

Hard-shell clams, specifically quahogs, are a wonderfully tasting species of mollusk found in the United States and typically used in this classic chowder.

Serves 4
6¾ lb hard-shell clams, 10 teaspoons butter
⅔ cup finely diced uncooked, smoked bacon
¾ cup finely chopped onion, ⅓ cup flour
3¼ cups milk
1¼ cups carrots, diced into ½-inch pieces
kernels from 8½ oz fresh corn (about 2 ears)
1¼ lb potatoes, cut into ½-inch cubes
⅔ cup leeks, sliced into thin rings
⅞ cup thinly sliced celery
½ cup cream
salt, freshly ground white pepper
For the garnish:
1 tablespoon chopped parsley

Wash the clams well under cold water, then let dry. To open, hold firmly in one hand and insert the blade of a sturdy knife between the top and bottom shells, easing the knife along with a rotating motion. Cut through the muscle in the top shell and continue on up to the hinge, opening all the clams this way, and reserving the liquid they release. Separate the meat from the bottom shell, remove, and set aside. Melt the butter in a pot, and briefly sauté the bacon. Add the onion and sauté until translucent. Sprinkle in the flour and continue sautéing, stirring frequently, until lightly browned. Proceed as shown in the picture sequence below. Stir the cream in last and season with salt and pepper. Garnish with parsley and serve.

Simmer the thickened bacon-onion mixture with the clam sauce for several minutes, stirring occasionally.

Pour in the milk, stirring constantly, and slowly simmer over low to medium heat.

Stir in the carrots, corn kernels, and potatoes, and simmer for 20 minutes.

Add the leeks, celery, and clams, and simmer for another 10 minutes.

Mixed-bean soup

A hearty bean stew with chicken, using a homemade broth

This five-bean stew is quite tasty made with chicken, but fish may also be substituted with no loss of flavor. In this case, use a fish stock as a base, and well-seasoned, fried cubes of fresh tuna as a nice, firm, garnish. In either case, the dish is rounded out with a spoonful of chopped epazote, an herb with a delicate citrus flavor that is very popular in Mexico. Bean preparation also remains the same, although the cooking times will vary according to the variety of the bean: Borlotti, small white beans, pinto beans, and kidney beans take 40–45 minutes; scarlet runners, 50 minutes.

Serves 4
3½ oz each dried pinto and Borlotti beans
3½ oz each dried kidney and scarlet runner beans
3½ oz dried small, white beans (e.g., pea beans)
7½ teaspoons butter
¾ cup shallots, sliced into thin rings
1½ oz fresh ginger, cut into 3 pieces
1 chile pepper, halved lengthwise
10 teaspoons lemon juice
2 lime leaves, salt, freshly ground pepper
For the chicken broth:
1 boiling chicken, giblets removed (about 2¼ lb)
1¼ lb veal bones, cut into sections
¾ cup diced carrots, ½ cup diced leeks
½ cup diced celery
1 crushed garlic clove
½ onion studded with 2 whole cloves
10 white peppercorns, 1 bay leaf
1 thyme sprig, 2 parsley stalks
For the garnish:
1 tablespoon chopped epazote or cilantro

A wide variety of beans is combined in this recipe — just the right meal after a long day of hard work — especially since it is easy to prepare. Once the broth is ready and the beans are soft, the rest is simple.

1. Rinse the different beans separately under cold water. Place in separate bowls with enough cold water to cover and let soak overnight. The next day, pour off the water and cook the beans separately until soft (see above), then drain well and set aside.

2. To make about 6½ cups of chicken broth, wash the chicken inside and out under cold water, drain, and cut into quarters. Place the chicken and veal bones in a large pot with enough hot water to cover and quickly bring to a boil, doing so until the protein and impurities rise to the surface. Remove from heat, drain, and rinse the

chicken and veal bones in warm water. Return both to the pot, cover with about 9 cups of fresh water, and bring to a boil again, repeatedly skimming off the scum that rises to the surface. Reduce heat and simmer at just under boiling point for about 3 hours.

3. After 2 hours, add the carrots, leeks, celery, garlic, onion, peppercorns, bay leaf, thyme, and parsley to the pot and simmer, adding water if necessary. After 3 hours, remove the chicken (set aside) and veal bones (discard), strain the broth through a piece of cheesecloth into a pot, then let cool and skim off the fat. Set aside.

4. Melt the butter and sauté the shallots until translucent. Add the ginger, chile pepper, lemon juice, and lime leaves and sauté briefly. Pour in 4½ cups of the prepared broth and bring to a boil. Reduce heat and simmer for 30 minutes. Remove the lime leaves, ginger, and chile pepper. Add the drained beans and simmer for another 10 minutes. Keep warm.

5. Skin the chicken, separate the meat from the bones, and cut it into bite-sized pieces. Add these to the soup and heat through; season with salt and pepper. Ladle into warmed bowls, garnish with the epazote or cilantro, and serve.

Roasted red-pepper soup

An intriguing combination: grilled sweet peppers and the delicate, aniseed flavor of fennel cream

Serves 4

1¾ lb sweet red peppers, cut into quarters

2 tablespoons vegetable oil

7½ teaspoons butter, 1½ cups finely chopped onion

2 finely chopped hot red peppers

½ oz sliced fresh ginger

3¼ cups chicken stock, dash lime juice

pinch sugar, salt, freshly ground white pepper

For the fennel cream:

2 oz finely chopped fennel

¼ teaspoon crushed fennel seeds

½ cup chicken stock, ¾ cup cream

salt, 1 tablespoon chopped fennel leaves

2 teaspoons Pernod (French liqueur)

You will also need:

1½ oz thinly shaved fennel, fennel leaves

1. Brush the sweet peppers with vegetable oil, and brown thoroughly until the skin blisters. Place in a plastic bag and steam for 10 minutes, then peel off the skin (discarding it). Dice ½ cup of the skinned peppers, reserving for later, and chop the remainder into small pieces.

2. Melt the butter and sauté the onion until translucent. Add the chopped sweet peppers, hot peppers, and ginger, and sauté for 5 minutes. Pour in the chicken stock and bring to a boil. Reduce heat and simmer, covered, for 1 hour. Remove from heat, purée, and strain. Season with lime juice, sugar, salt, and pepper and set aside.

3. For the fennel cream, boil together the fennel, and the chicken stock. Reduce heat and simmer until all the liquid has evaporated. Add the cream and simmer for another 10 minutes. Remove from heat, purée, and strain well. Season with salt and let cool. Stir in the fennel leaves and Pernod. Chill thoroughly and whip the fennel cream until it forms soft peaks.

4. Add the reserved sweet peppers to the soup. Reheat and ladle into 4 bowls. Serve with the fennel cream, shaved fennel, and fennel leaves.

Perfectly ripened: When bell peppers are left long enough on the plant, they turn red and develop their maximum vitamin C content.

Sweet-corn soup
Served with small, crispy crab cakes

Corn, one of the most important foods of Native Americans, was completely unknown to the Europeans when they arrived here long ago. Nowadays, corn is a staple food all over the country. In addition to cornbread and cornmeal pasta, fresh corn is used in numerous other recipes; many soup dishes, for example, list corn kernels as an ingredient. In this recipe, kernels from the ubiquitous, green-husked sweet corn — blended until smooth and enriched with cream — serve as the basis of this delicate, creamy soup.

Serves 4
For the corn soup:
6 tablespoons butter
2 ears of fresh sweet corn (about 1¼ lb), in their husks

Preheat the oven to 350°. Wrap the corn in aluminum foil and place in an ovenproof dish; bake for 90 minutes. Remove from the oven and let cool slightly.

Unwrap the corn from the foil and remove the husks and silk. Holding firmly by the stalk, cut the kernels off close to the cob with a sharp knife and set aside.

Crab cakes are especially popular on the East Coast where crabbing is a popular pastime. There, crab cakes are made from the meat of freshly caught blue crabs.

½ cup leeks (white part only), chopped into small pieces
⅔ cup diced onion, ⅓ cup diced celeriac
3¼ cups fish stock
1⅛ cups cream, salt, freshly ground white pepper
For the crab cakes:
3½ oz crabmeat
5½ oz finely diced bell peppers (red, green, yellow)
8 teaspoons finely diced celery
¼ finely chopped, red chile pepper
1 tablespoon chopped parsley
2 tablespoons mayonnaise, ⅓ cup white bread crumbs
salt, freshly ground pepper, 1 teaspoon lemon juice
· 7½ teaspoons butter for frying
For the garnish:
chopped parsley leaves

1. Melt 7½ teaspoons of butter. Wash the corn, drain well, and brush with the melted butter. Proceed as shown in the picture sequence opposite.

2. To make the crab cakes, remove any bits of cartilage or shell from the crabmeat. Place the bell peppers, celery, chile pepper, parsley, mayonnaise, bread crumbs, and crabmeat in a bowl; mix thoroughly; and season with salt, pepper, and lemon juice. Cover and refrigerate for about an hour.

3. To prepare the soup, melt the remaining butter in a pot and sauté the leeks, onion, and celeriac for 5 minutes. Add the corn kernels and sauté briefly. Pour in the fish stock and bring to a boil. Reduce heat and simmer, covered, for 40 minutes. Stir in the cream, season with salt and pepper, and simmer for another 15 minutes. Remove from heat, purée in a blender, and strain through a fine-mesh sieve. Set aside.

4. In the meantime, shape the crabmeat mixture into 8 balls of equal size; press flat. Melt the butter in a frying pan and fry the crab cakes for 2 minutes on each side.

5. Reheat the soup, ladle into 4 bowls, place 2 crab cakes in each, garnish with parsley, and serve.

Tabasco production:
This concentrated, diabolically hot sauce — only a drop or two is needed for seasoning — is brewed in large fermenting vats on Avery Island in the Mississippi River delta from red chile peppers, wine vinegar, and salt.

Crawfish stew

A hot and spicy shellfish and rice dish from the South

The swamplands of the Mississippi and Louisiana bayous provide the ideal habitat for crawfish. It is no coincidence that this area has a long-standing tradition of recipes featuring this, and other shellfish.

Serves 4
4½ lb crawfish, salt
For the crawfish stock:
4 tablespoons vegetable oil
2¼ cups coarsely diced onion
12½ oz tomatoes, chopped into small pieces
2 tablespoons tomato paste
¼ cup celery, chopped into small pieces
5 garlic cloves, halved lengthwise
1 bay leaf, 5 white peppercorns, ½ teaspoon salt
For the stew:
¼ cup vegetable oil, ⅓ cup flour
¾ cup long-grain rice, salt, freshly ground pepper
2 cups finely chopped onion, 2 finely chopped garlic cloves
1 cup diced celery
7 oz green peppers, cut into ¼-inch pieces
⅔ cup scallions, cut into thin rings
dash Tabasco sauce
For the garnish:
2 tablespoons chopped parsley, parsley stalks

Rice, another product of the South, is also featured in this piquantly seasoned, tasty stew – proving once again Southerners' love of good food.

1. Preheat the oven to 390–400°. Add the crawfish to a pot of lightly salted, boiling water one after another, and cook 3–4 minutes each, making sure that the water comes back to a roiling boil before adding the next crawfish. Remove with a slotted spoon and plunge briefly in cold water. To extract the meat from the shell, twist the tail off the body, taking care to leave the tail meat as intact as possible. Devein and refrigerate the tails. Halve the bodies lengthwise, remove the insides and discard. Wash the shells thoroughly under cold water to get rid of any remaining debris and let drain. Place the cleaned shells on a baking sheet and roast for 1 hour.

2. To prepare the crawfish stock, heat the vegetable oil in a large pot and sauté the onion. Add the crawfish shells and continue to sauté.

Stir in the tomatoes and tomato paste. Add the celery, garlic, bay leaf, peppercorns, and salt. Pour in 10½ cups of water and bring to a boil. Reduce heat and simmer for 1½ hours, skimming off any scum that rises to the surface. Remove from heat. Line a conical sieve with a piece of cheesecloth, gradually pour in the stock, and let run through. Set aside.

3. For the stew, heat 8 teaspoons of vegetable oil in a large pot and sprinkle in the flour, heating until it turns light brown, stirring continuously. Slowly add the prepared crawfish stock, stirring frequently, then bring to a boil. Lower the heat

and reduce the stock to about 6½ cups, stirring occasionally. If the stock becomes lumpy, push it through a sieve. Add the rice, season with salt and pepper, and simmer for 10 minutes.

4. Heat the remaining vegetable oil in a frying pan and sauté the onion and garlic without letting them brown. Add the celery and green peppers, and sauté for 5 minutes. Transfer the contents of the frying pan to the crawfish stock and simmer for 10 minutes. Add the scallions and crawfish tails, and simmer for another 5 minutes. Season with Tabasco, and serve garnished with the parsley.

Chorizo, the soft, Spanish sausage made from coarsely chopped meat, is usually lightly smoked and seasoned with chile peppers, garlic, and paprika.

Jambalaya

This hot-chile, Creole rice stew has become very popular not only throughout the United States, but elsewhere in the world

This recipe originated in the South, where rice cultivation has a tradition stretching back over a century. Although rice was formerly grown almost exclusively in North and South Carolina, today California, Arizona, and Louisiana are important rice-producing states. In the South, they still have a particular passion for Jambalaya, a dish that has almost an infinite number of variations. Occasionally, the entire seafood harvest from the Gulf of Mexico — shrimp, crayfish, oysters, and lobsters — is added to the stew. On the other hand, a land-based variant can be prepared, like the one here with pork, chorizo (Spanish sausage), and wild mushrooms.

Serves 4
1½ oz pork lard
2¼ lb pork leg, cut into ½-inch cubes
8½ oz chorizo, skinned and sliced into thin rounds
2½ cups finely chopped onion
5 finely chopped garlic cloves
1 cup diced celery
10½ oz sweet red peppers, diced into ¼-inch pieces
1 red chile pepper, diced into ¼-inch pieces
2¼ cups long-grain rice
4½–6½ cups meat stock
salt, freshly ground pepper
8½ oz wild mushrooms, cut into bite-sized pieces
¾ cup scallions, cut into rings
For the garnish:
2 tablespoons chopped parsley

1. Heat the lard in a medium-sized pot and brown the pork meat all over for about 20–25 minutes. Add the sausage and brown for 5 minutes, stirring frequently. Mix in the onion, garlic, celery, and sweet peppers, and simmer over medium heat for 5 minutes.

2. Stir in the chile pepper and the rice. Pour in some of the meat stock, season with salt and pepper, and bring to a boil. Reduce heat and simmer for 20 minutes. Pour in as much of the remaining meat stock as needed to make the stew moist, but not soggy.

3. Add the mushrooms and scallions last, and simmer for another 5 minutes. Adjust the seasonings, garnish with parsley, and serve.

With the help of a metal ring or coffee can, it's easy to get the proper height when cutting off the pumpkin lid. Using a sharp knife, cut all the way around in a zigzag pattern, using the ring as a guide, then lift off the lid.

Corn and pumpkin soup

Typically American in its ingredients, with a hot-chile twist

American cuisine would be unimaginable today without the gourd family in all its variations. Different forms of these basic, viny plants were known to Native Americans, including summer and winter squash (of which the pumpkin is one). Having a fairly unobtrusive taste of its own, pumpkin is suitable in a wide range of dishes — as a basis for cakes, chutneys, and purées, or for puddings and casseroles. Well-seasoned pumpkin soups are also very popular. The first European settlers learned how to prepare the latter from Native Americans, who were masters at cooking tasty pumpkin stews. Instead of a pot, they would use the hollowed-out pumpkin shells, which they simply placed in hot coals to cook. The soup recipe given below, containing carrots and onion in addition to pumpkin and corn, can be served in the hollowed-out pumpkin shell if desired; however, it is of course easier to cook on the stove.

This creamy corn and pumpkin soup looks especially attractive served in its original packaging — the hollowed-out pumpkin.

Serves 4
1 small pumpkin (about 3½ lb)
4 tablespoons corn oil
¾ cup finely chopped onion
1 cup carrots, diced into ¼-inch pieces
kernels from 2 ears of corn (about 7 oz each)
1 finely chopped red chile pepper (save the seeds)
6½ cups vegetable stock
salt, freshly ground white pepper
For the garnish:
1 tablespoon chopped peppermint

1. Carefully peel the pumpkin using a sharp knife or vegetable peeler. Scoop out the seeds and fibrous material from the center, and cut the remaining core into ¼-inch pieces. Set aside. (The pumpkin seeds can be rinsed, dried, and eaten raw, or salted and roasted if desired.)

2. Heat the corn oil in a pot and sauté the onion until translucent. Add the carrots and pumpkin and sauté briefly. Add the corn kernels, chile pepper, (and reserved seeds for a spicier taste), and vegetable stock; season with salt and pepper; and bring to a boil. Reduce heat and simmer,

covered, for about 25 minutes. Remove from heat, purée, and strain through a fine-mesh sieve. If the soup is too thick, add a little vegetable stock. Reheat, adjust the seasonings, garnish with the peppermint, and serve.

3. If desired, the soup may be served in its pumpkin shell. To do this, cut off the top third in a zigzag pattern, using a sharp knife and a ring or coffee can (as shown at the top of page 204) before removing the contents. After preparing the soup, lift off the lid, fill with the hot soup, and serve immediately.

Preparing the closed flowers. The flowers need not be opened to remove the pistil; hold the flower firmly in one hand and twist out the sepals, together with the pistil, with the other.

Zucchini-flower soup

Distinctive in both color and flavor, with a delicate garnish of fried chicken breast and mushrooms

It is not just the slender fruit of the zucchini squash that is considered suitable for eating — sometimes the bright yellow flowers are also used in more refined dishes. In this recipe, they form the basis of the soup, along with the green vegetable. If a sufficient quantity of zucchini flowers is not available — either at the store or from the garden — half of the given amount can be replaced with pumpkin flowers.

Serves 4

10½ oz zucchini, 3½ oz zucchini flowers
7½ teaspoons butter
¼ cup sliced scallions; 2 sliced garlic cloves
1 small thinly sliced jalapeño pepper
1 tablespoon chopped parsley, thyme, and tarragon
3½ cups chicken stock
salt, freshly ground pepper
1 tablespoon heavy cream blended with dash of buttermilk (crème fraîche)
For the garnish:
1½ oz zucchini flowers, 7½ teaspoons butter
7 oz chicken breast, sliced into ½-inch-wide strips
4½ oz sliced mushrooms, salt
freshly ground pepper, 1 tablespoon chopped parsley

Proceed as shown in the first three steps of the picture sequence opposite. Melt the butter in a pot and sauté the scallions and garlic without letting them brown, then stir in the jalapeño pepper. Add the zucchini pieces and flowers and sauté briefly, sprinkle in the herbs, pour in the chicken stock, and proceed as shown in the 4th photo. When the zucchini is tender, purée the soup with a handheld blender, stir in the crème fraîche, adjust the seasonings, and keep hot. For the garnish, prepare the zucchini flowers as described above, then cut into strips. Melt the butter in a frying pan and brown the chicken

breast thoroughly. Proceed as shown in the 5th photo. Season with salt and pepper and sprinkle in the parsley. Ladle the soup into bowls, and serve with the prepared garnish.

Cut off both ends of the zucchini and slice into even, medium-sized pieces. Set aside.

Prepare the open flowers as follows: First, use scissors to snip out the pistil.

Next, cut off the tip of the stalk and the sepals, and slice the flowers crosswise into thin strips. Set aside.

Season with salt and pepper and bring to a boil. Reduce heat and simmer for about 15 minutes.

Add the mushrooms and sauté for 1–2 minutes. Add the flowers and sauté for a few more seconds.

Callaloo harvest in Jamaica. The green leaves are not the only part of this plant to be prized as a culinary treat — the starchy tubers also are a staple food in the Caribbean, as well as in other tropical regions where callaloo grows.

Jamaican pepper pot

Quintessentially Caribbean: a soup with callaloo, chayote (a member of the gourd family), coconut milk, and Scotch bonnet chile peppers

Callaloo (in French, *calalou*) is a member of the Arum family, found in tropical marshlands. The leaves of the plant, unfortunately, are hard to find, but Swiss chard makes a good substitute, both in appearance and flavor. If preferred, the soup may be served with wheat flour "dumplin's" — a popular accompaniment in the West Indies — instead of noodles. To make the sophisticated-looking variation suggested here, knead together 1½ cups of flour with a little salt and enough water (about 4 tablespoons) to make a soft dough. Shape the mixture into thin, 1½-inch-long rolls that taper to a point at both ends. Add these to the soup 15 minutes before the end of cooking time.

Serves 4
1 fresh coconut
10½ oz callaloo or Swiss chard
2 whole garlic cloves
2 oz uncooked bacon (about 3 slices)
1 cup carrots, cut into ¼-inch pieces
5½ oz chayote, cut into ¼-inch pieces
7 oz mealy potatoes, cut into ½-inch pieces
1 whole scallion, 3 thyme sprigs
1 whole green Scotch bonnet pepper, salt
1 oz soup noodles
You will also need:
thyme leaves, 4 Scotch bonnet peppers for the garnish

The basic ingredients — bacon, vegetables, and noodles — are simmered in this dark-green, creamy soup. The last-minute addition of the Scotch bonnet pepper provides a nice kick.

1. First, prepare the coconut: Puncture two of the three "eyes" at the flatter end with a hammer and nail and pour the liquid into a bowl. Then, open the coconut — most easily done by sawing into it with a sharp saw and cracking it open with a hammer. Break off the hard, outer shell in

pieces, then remove the thin, brown skin from the meat with a potato peeler. Dice the meat, and purée in a blender with the reserved liquid. If needed, add water to made 2⅛ cups of coconut milk. Set aside.

2. Remove the coarse stalks from the callaloo greens, and string the finer ones. Thoroughly wash the stalks and leaves and dice.

3. Bring 3¼ cups of water to a boil in a pot, and stir in the callaloo, garlic, bacon, and 1½ cups of prepared coconut milk. Cover and simmer for 10 minutes. Remove from heat and let cool slightly.

Remove the bacon, purée in a blender, and return to the pot along with the bacon.

4. Stir in the carrots, chayote, and potatoes. Add the scallion, thyme, and the Scotch bonnet pepper, then pour in the remaining coconut milk. Season with salt and simmer, covered, for 20 minutes.

5. Stir in the noodles and simmer for another 5 minutes. Remove the thyme sprigs, scallion, and the pepper. Adjust the seasonings, ladle into 4 bowls, and serve garnished with thyme leaves and 1 Scotch bonnet pepper per bowl.

Scotch bonnet peppers like the ones on sale at this market in Ocho Rios in Jamaica are recognizable by their broad, highly wrinkled pods. Their skin is so thin that they look almost translucent — but their main claim to fame is their infernal heat.

Pumpkin soup

A simple soup, but thoroughly delectable when made with the proper squash

Butternut squash — the variety called for in the original Jamaican recipe — is the ideal kind of squash for this soup. It is a type of winter squash, which includes the pumpkin, and is distinguished by its aromatic, carotene-rich pulp. Butternut squash, moreover, is also soft as butter and has a nutty flavor — hence its (self-explanatory) name — and can be found on Thanksgiving dinner tables around the country. The fruit — botanically speaking, a berry — looks like a somewhat ungainly bottle; the seeds are only found in the "paunchy" part. It is also very popular in the Caribbean and is easy to find in grocery stores (or fresh from the garden in the later summer months).

Serves 4
2 tablespoons vegetable oil
⅔ cup finely chopped onion
1 finely chopped garlic clove
½ cup scallions, sliced into rings
2¼ lb butternut squash, cut into ¾-inch chunks
½ seeded Scotch bonnet pepper
3 thyme sprigs
1 bay leaf, salt
For the garnish:
¼ cup scallions, cut into thin rings
1 teaspoon thyme leaves

1. Heat the vegetable oil in a pot and sauté the onion, garlic, and scallions without letting them brown. Add the squash and sauté for another 4–5 minutes.

The garnish of scallions and thyme adds plenty of flavor, deliciously rounding out this soup, which owes its creaminess to the puréed butternut squash.

2. Pour in 4½ cups of water and bring to a boil. Add the Scotch bonnet pepper, thyme sprigs, and bay leaf, and season with salt.

3. Reduce heat and simmer for 25–30 minutes. Remove the thyme sprigs and bay leaf. Take out the pepper also, if a less-fiery soup is preferred.

4. Remove from heat, finely purée in a blender or food processor, and strain through a fine-mesh

sieve. Return the soup to the pot, adjust the seasonings, and reheat.

5. Ladle the soup into warmed bowls, garnish with the scallions and thyme leaves, and serve right away.

Gadgets and Utensils

Most soups and stews can be easily prepared with the utensils and equipment found in the average kitchen. For clear soups, various sieves and straining cloths (such as cheesecloth) are indispensable; and for many cream soups, a food processor, mixer, or handheld blender is a requirement. The additional utensils shown here are useful, if not essential kitchen accoutrements.

1 Conical sieve
2 Straining cloth
3 Soup kettle
4 Wok
5 Oriental slotted spoon
6 Stockpot
7 Braising pot
8 Mixing bowls
9 Stainless steel saucepans
10 Sieves
11 Measuring cup
12 Mixer
13 Handheld blender
14 Chopper with chopping board
15 Electric mixer
16 Slotted spoon
17 Ladle
18 Sauce spoon
19 Spatula
20 Mortar and pestle
21 Juicer
22 Lobster pliers
23 Poultry shears
24 Kitchen scissors
25 Melon ballers
26 Citrus peeler
27 Vegetable knife
28 Vegetable peeler
29 Asparagus peeler
30 Garlic press
31 All-purpose knife
32 Kitchen knives
33 Carving knife
34 Carving fork
35 Chef's knife

Index

References to information on ingredients or techniques are given in italics. All other entries refer to recipes.